THE FIRST AMENDMENT

AN ILLUSTRATED HISTORY

ROBERT J. McWHIRTER

Published in the United States by Constitution Press
an imprint of RR&G Enterprises LLC
PO Box 26666
Tempe Arizona 85285

Originally published in the United States as
Chapter 1 of *Bills, Quills, and Stills; An Annotated, Illustrated, and Illuminated History of the Bill of Rights.*

Distributed in the United States by Applewood Books
1 River Road
Carlisle, MA 01741
toll free: 800-277-5312
main: 781-271-0055

For bulk purchases for associations and other large groups,
please contact Applewood Books.

Library of Congress Control Number: 2017933501

ISBN: 978-1-945682-03-2

Design and layout of text by Quadrum Solutions

A high school kid unfurled a banner at an off-campus school activity reading,

"Bong Hits 4 Jesus." [1]

He got suspended for ten days and eventually lost his case in the U.S. Supreme Court. [2]

But was it speech or religion? Actually, it doesn't matter—it was the First Amendment.

Speech *and* religion! People fight wars about either, and especially about both, including the American Revolution. In fact, the kid got his suspension increased from five to ten days after he quoted Thomas Jefferson. [3]

1. Image by Helen Koop

Original Banner at the Newseum in Washington D.C.

2. *Morse v. Frederick*, 551 U.S. 393 (2007), held that the suspension did not violate the student's right to free speech, nor did confiscating the banner. The kid, Joseph Frederick, later settled his case just before the Alaskan Supreme Court was to decide it under the Alaskan Constitution. So, in Alaska at least, it appears that even a high school student can speak about or believe in *"Bong Hits 4 Jesus"*!

3. *Frederick v. Morse*, 439 F.3d 1114, 1116 (9th Cir. 2006). Jefferson had very clear ideas about Jesus, but he probably never used a bong.

Thomas Jefferson

A bong or water pipe is a smoking device for cannabis, tobacco, or other substances. The water cools the smoke.

"Congress shall make no law respecting an establishment of religion, or prohibiting the free exercise thereof; or abridging the freedom of speech, or of the press; or the right of the people peaceably to assemble, and to petition the Government for a redress of grievances."

—The First Amendment

As "*Bong Hits 4 Jesus*" shows, the First Amendment is front and center in the "culture debates." On any given topic—school prayer, "faith-based initiatives," abortion, the death penalty, health care, the Ten Commandments on public property—we debate the First Amendment's scope, both as to what we believe and what we can say about it.

But guess what? The First Amendment wasn't originally first. It started out as the third amendment. (So much for the hortatory speeches that "*the First Amendment is so important because the Framers put it first!*"). In fact, the Framers originally put it after an amendment regarding the size of the Congress and another related to Congress's pay.[1]

Our current First Amendment, though, was the first that articulated individual rights, and thus was always the start of the "Bill of Rights."[2] Even so, our modern understanding of freedom of speech and of the press is less than one hundred years old.[3] And as we will see, the Framers, for the most part, would not have considered the First Amendment the main definer of religious freedom and free speech.

This is not the case today.

Under the First Amendment's Free Press, Speech,

---

1. See Anthony Lewis, Freedom for the Thought That We Hate: A Biography of the First Amendment 9 (2007). The original "first amendment" concerning the size of the House of Representatives and congressional apportionment never passed, but the states did ratify the original "second amendment" concerning congressional salaries on May 7, 1992, making it the Twenty-Seventh Amendment: "*No law, varying the compensation for the services of the Senators and Representatives, shall take effect until an election of Representatives shall have intervened.*" U.S. Const. amend. XXVII).

James Madison

2. The First Amendment was James Madison's personal project. Brent Tarter, *Virginians and the Bill of Rights*, in The Bill of Rights: A Lively Heritage 12 (Jon Kukla ed., 1987). He gets credit for being the "father of the Bill of Rights" because he made a campaign promise to get it passed and sifted through piles of proposals and wording to do so. See **Prequel and Preamble: Did They Just Forget to Pay the Bill?**

3. Before World War I, the courts generally did not protect speech. Not until *Gitlow v. New York*, 268 U.S. 652 (1925), did the Supreme Court hold that the First Amendment applied to the states. *Near v. Minnesota*, 283 U.S. 697 (1931), was the first time the Supreme Court ruled for the press against a prior restraint by holding unconstitutional a state statute enjoining publication of an allegedly defamatory newspaper. That same year, the Supreme Court upheld the validity of symbolic speech in *Stromberg v. California*, 283 U.S. 359 (1931), by invali- dating a California law that forbade the display of a red flag "*as a sign, symbol or emblem of opposition to organized government.*" It took until 1965 for the Court to hold unconstitutional a federal law as violating the First Amendment in *Lamont v. Postmaster General*, 381 U.S. 301 (1965). *See, e.g.*, David M. Rabban, *The Emergence of Modern First Amendment Doctrine*, 50 U. Chi. L. Rev. 1205, 1213–15 (1983). *See* Lewis 112–23 (discussing the lack of court protection to violations of speech and religious rights for most of American history; *see also* David M. O'Brien, *Freedom of Speech and Free Govern-* ment: *The First Amendment, the Supreme Court and the Polity*, in The Bill of Rights: A Lively Heritage 43, 48, 52 (Jon Kukla ed., 1987) (noting that the First Amendment shows two hundred years of expansion). For the growth of the First Amendment in the courts, *see* Floyd Abrams, Speaking Freely: Trials of the First Amendment (2005); Erwin Chemerinsky, *History, Tradition, the Supreme Court, and the First Amendment*, 44 Hastings L.J. 901, 916 (1993) (noting that the tradition of protecting speech and religion has changed profoundly over time).

Petition, and Assembly Clauses, people print, blog, speak out, protest, petition, argue, and march.[4] People are motivated to do all that printing, blogging, speaking, protesting, petitioning, arguing, and marching by their respective creeds. They demand to freely exercise their creed *and* to be free from someone else establishing a different creed over them.

In this sense, the First Amendment's two com-ponents of speech and religion define us. No other part of the Constitution has this scope.[5]

Both the political Left and political Right hold free speech as an article of faith, and whole political movements, such as the Moral Majority and the civil rights movement, have organized around religion.[6]

Although the First Amendment's current scope is a modern innovation, the aspiration it embodies and the rights it incorporates are products of history— and a rich history at that.

In fact, the kid with the *"Bong Hits 4 Jesus"* banner—a little turning point in history—now has something in common with Sir Thomas More, who in 1535 defied King Henry VIII—a big fat turning point in history.

"I die the King's good servant and God's first."

4. *"Stop the Presses!"* The press itself often becomes "the story" in movies that range from the suspense drama ALL THE PRESIDENT'S MEN, (Warner Brothers, 1976) about Watergate, to the comedy-drama THE PAPER, (Universal Pictures, 1994) in which the main character gets to yell, *"Stop the Presses!"* And of course, there is Orson Welles' masterpiece (and perhaps the best American movie of all time), CITIZEN KANE (RKO Pictures 1941), a fictional account of William Randolph Hearst and his newspaper empire. For a discussion of Hearst and "yellow" journalism, see Trevor D. Dryer, *"All the News That's Fit to Print": The New York Times, "Yellow" Journalism, and the Criminal Trial 1898–1902,* 8 NEV. L. J. 541 (2008).

5. *"The First Amendment is truly the heart of the Bill of Rights."* Hugo L. Black, *The Bill of Rights,* 35 N.Y.U. L. REV. 865, 881 (1960). *"Nothing that I have read in the Congressional debates on the Bill of Rights indicates that there was any belief that the First Amendment contained any qualifications."* *Id.* at 880.

6. King stating the dream.

So said More—knight, lawyer, judge, and once lord chancellor of England—just before King Henry VIII had his head chopped off.

Sure, More's statement is literally graver than the kid's "*Bong Hits 4 Jesus*," but it is still about stating a creed.

A lot of people died for religion then, as they continue to do now. So what makes More special?

Aside from the fact that A MAN FOR ALL SEASONS is a great movie,[1] More represents the confluence of the First Amendment's two parts: speech and religion, the same as "*Bong Hits 4 Jesus*."

Ironically, it was not what More said that got him killed; it was what he refused to say. Specifically, he refused to swear an oath, the Act of Supremacy, regarding Henry's hostile takeover of the Catholic Church

in England.[2] Speech, like religion, can be symbolic as well as spoken.

Henry killed a lot of people for speaking about such things.

That More lost his head for something he did not say is ironic because he was the greatest speaker of his day.[3] Henry knew this and sent a message to More that

"[t]he King's pleasure is further that at your

Henry VIII

1. A MAN FOR ALL SEASONS (Columbia Pictures 1966) won an Academy Award for Best Picture. Robert Bolt adapted his stage play for the movie. Courts have quoted both the film and play numerous times, including the U.S. Supreme Court in *National Ass'n of Home Builders v. Defenders of Wildlife*, 551 U.S. 644 (2007). Robert Bolt's final film project was his screenplay for THE MISSION (Warner Brothers 1986), which picked up on the themes of moral conscience and religion presented in A MAN FOR ALL SEASONS twenty years earlier.

2. See **Chapter 5 of *Bills, Quills, and Stills*, (Constitution Press re-release 2017)**, discussing More's role in the history of the right to remain silent.

Sir Thomas More

execution you shall not use many words."[4]

"I die the King's good servant and God's first."

Today we effectively view the First Amendment as *two* amendments: one regarding religion and another regarding speech. But the First Amendment actually emerged from the interplay between the two.

It was not enough that Henry arranged to "legally" kill More; Henry also did not want an embarrassing execution.[5]

They were more than enough.

But though Henry could count on More's obedience to be brief, More knew the value of a good sound-bite. Aside from a few customary quips and exchanges, such as forgiving his executioner, More said only the words quoted above.

The best speeches are often the shortest, and in just nine words More summed up the whole conflict about the right to say what you believe without government reprisal.[6] Although the confluence of speech and religion undid him, his words live on to indict Henry.

Henry's break with the Roman Catholic Church, part of the Protestant Reformation, illustrates this interplay; what you believed and what you said about it became a government problem.[7]

---

3. In happier times, More had been speaker of the House of Commons and stood his ground against Cardinal Wolsey, who as lord chancellor and papal legate exercised both the power of the young King Henry and that of the faraway pope.

As we shall see, in 1523, Sir More wrote a PETITION FOR FREE SPEECH to Henry, arguing that the king was better served by a Parliament that did not fear reprisal from open and frank discussion of differing points of view.

Thomas More Defending the Liberty of the House of Commons by Vivian Forbes

4. More's son-in-law, William Roper, wrote of More's death about twenty years later. WILLIAM ROPER, THE LIFE OF SIR THOMAS MORE c. 1556–57 (Gerard B. Wegemer & Stephen W. Smith eds., 2003), *available at* http://www.thomasmorestudies.org/docs/Roper.pdf.

5. As Justice Hugo Black wrote, "[m]*isuse of government power, particularly in times of stress, has brought suffering to humanity in all ages about which we have authentic history. Some of the world's noblest and finest men have suffered ignominy and death for no crime—unless unorthodoxy is a crime.*" Black at 879.

6. More did not become Saint Thomas More until Pope Pius XI canonized him in 1935. What he had to "say" about Henry, conscience, and political power applies just as well to totalitarianism under Hitler, Stalin, and Mussolini.

Contrary to popular belief, More is not the patron saint of lawyers—that is Saint Ives—but of statesmen.

Pope Pius XI

Saint Ives (Ivo of Kermartin, canonized in June 1347 by Pope Clement VI), whose prayer reads:

"Saint Yvo was a lawyer, and not a thief, A thing almost beyond belief."

7. A contemporary engraving showing **Henry VIII** (already getting fat) enthroned on top of Pope Clement, with Bishop Fisher trying to help the pope and Henry's new archbishop of Canterbury, Thomas Cramner, and new lord chancellor, Thomas Cromwell, supporting the king. The scene also shows Henry binding over monks for execution and confiscating the wealth of the church. All of this happens while Cramner hands Henry the printed Word, connecting religion and press.

Henry *established* himself as the pope in England and the Anglican Church as the official religion, which is why we have an *anti*-establishment clause that

"Congress shall make no law respecting an establishment of religion . . . ." [1]

But Henry and his successors had no idea what they had gotten themselves into, because in breaking with Rome, they not only had to suppress Catholics[2] but all manner of dissenters from established Anglicanism, most notably Puritans.[3] This is why we have a "free exercise" clause that

"Congress shall make no law . . . prohibiting the free exercise thereof [religion] .."

The dissenters, however, would not keep their mouths shut despite the crown's and the established church's best efforts to suppress them. They spoke out, and the Anglicans tried them, which

1. Religion and Dogma. Even today, Americans are a religious people, but they are much less *dogmatic. See* Richard Albert, *Religion in the New Republic,* 67 LA. L. REV. 1, 22 (2006). America has seen, for instance, the growth of Protestant "megachurches" having little or no connection with any Protestant denomination or predefined doctrine.

"Dogma" is a given religion or other organization's undisputable belief or doctrine. In the religious context, divergence from it is "heresy." The word comes from Greek, and the plural is either "dogmas" or "dogmata." Denominations, sects, and organizations spend a lot of time defining dogma. The Catholic Church, for example, has different levels for defining dogma,

which as history shows leaves a lot of room for interpretation. *See, e.g., Dogma,* THE CATHOLIC ENCYCLOPEDIA, http://www.newadvent.org/cathen/05089a.htm (last visited Nov. 12, 2009). DOGMA (Miramax Films 1999) is an American adventure-comedy-fantasy satirizing the Catholic Church and belief.

Religion, though largely unknowable and impenetrable, is still central to most people. Albert at 8–9. Defining "religion" is difficult and attempts range from *"belief in the existence of a larger force; and adherence to a code of human conduct"* and *"[a] system of faith and worship usually involving belief in a supreme being and usually containing a moral or ethical code,"* to *"recognition on the part of man of some higher unseen power as control*

of his destiny, and as being entitled to obedience, reverence, and worship; the general mental and moral attitude resulting from this belief, with reference to its effect upon the individual or the Community" to *"the voluntary subjection of oneself to God"* to *"any belief system which serves the psychological function of alleviating death anxiety."* Albert at 10–11, *citing* BLACK'S LAW DICTIONARY 1293–94 (7th ed. 1999); XIII OXFORD ENGLISH DICTIONARY 568–69 (2d ed. 1989); XII CATHOLIC ENCYCLOPEDIA 739 (1909); James M. Donovan, *God Is as God Does: Law, Anthropology, and the Definition of "Religion,"* 6 SETON HALL CONST. L.J. 23, 95 (1995).

The Lakewood Megachurch interior in Houston, Texas

The Crystal Cathedral in Garden Grove, California

is why we have a freedom of speech clause that

"Congress shall make no law . . . abridging the freedom of speech . . . ." [4]

They continued to write pamphlets and books, and the kings continued to burn them—both the books and sometimes the Puritans—which is why we have a freedom of the press clause that

"Congress shall make no law . . . abridging the free-dom . . . of the press . . . ." [5]

They petitioned for rights, which the church and crown ignored, which is why we have the right to assemble and petition:

"Congress shall make no law . . . abridging the right of the people peaceably to assemble, and to petition the Government for a redress of grievances." [6]

---

2. Despite the admiration for More, anti-Catholicism became the norm in England. Catholicism went underground, which the story of Abbot Richard Whiting and his steward Thomas Horner shows.

Whiting was abbot of the great Glastonbury Abbey, built on the site of King Arthur's Avalon. In the early days of Henry VIII's stealing of church property, Whiting sent the king a pile of deeds to various manors in the abbey's possession. Because this did not occur in not an age of bank transfers, he sent the deeds hidden in a pie with his steward, Thomas Horner. The story is that Horner pulled out a deed for himself. What the record shows is that Horner testified against Whiting at his treason trial. Horner, for services to the crown, got the deed to the Manor of Mells, in Somerset, and a nursery rhyme:

™*Little Jack Horner sat in the corner, Eating a Christmas pie: He put in his thumb, and pulled out a plum, and said, 'What a good boy am I!'"*

Abbot Richard Whiting

3. The Pilgrims seeking a new world away from the established Church of England.

---

4. This includes a Puritan named **John Lilburne**, known as Freeborn John, who would not shut up! Lucky for us, he didn't. We will hear more about him in **Chapter 5: From Testicles to *Dragnet*: How the Fifth Amendment Protects *All* of Us** and **Chapter 6: How the Sixth Amendment Guarantees You a Court, a Lawyer, and a Chamber Pot.**

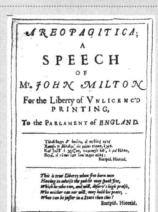

First page of AREOPAGITICA (1644)

THE PETITION OF RIGHT (1628)

Protesters assembling to demand jobs during the civil rights movement

5. The Puritan **John Milton**, who wrote the great epic poem PARADISE LOST (1667), first wrote one of the greatest defenses of free speech, AREOPAGITICA: A SPEECH OF MR. JOHN MILTON FOR THE LIBERTY OF UNLICENSED PRINTING TO THE PARLIAMENT OF ENGLAND (1644). We will hear more about Milton later in this chapter.

6. The Framers knew of Parliament's PETITION OF RIGHT (1628), setting out specific liberties that the king could not infringe: only Parliament could levy taxes, martial law could be imposed only during war, prisoners could challenge their detention through the writ of habeas corpus, and bans on the king's billeting troops in homes (the precursor of the Third Amendment). See **Chapter 3: The Third Amendment: Don't Count It Out Yet!**

We will return to Henry later because he is central to understanding why the Framers knew we needed the First Amendment.

The Framers also knew that fighting a revolution for rights, like those the First Amendment articulates, requires something to push the cause. Certainly the Enlightenment's promise of a free and open society motivated Jefferson, Adams, and Madison.

But for most of our history, especially the history the Founders knew, it was not a philosophy that pushed the struggle for rights, including the right to speak. It was religion.[1]

RELIGION AND SPEECH IN HISTORY

The Hebrews:

The ancients had a utilitarian approach to their gods. Treat them well, and the gods (supposedly) treated you well. They would not have understood the later Judeo-Christian idea that God is inherently good to *everyone*.[2]

---

1. The English and American experience refutes Karl Marx's pronouncement that "[r]eligion is the sign of the oppressed creature, the heart of a heartless world, and the soul of soulless conditions. It is the opium of the people."

Far from being the thing that oppressed people, religion and speech motivated them to gain rights and democracy. "They [the Framers] knew that free speech might be the friend of change and revolution. But they also knew that it is always the deadliest enemy of tyranny." Black at 881; Susan Wiltshire writes that free speech "does not ensure good government . . . [but] its absence does ensure totalitarianism." SUSAN FORD WILTSHIRE, GREECE, ROME, AND THE BILL OF RIGHTS 111 (1992); see also Walter B. Hamlin, The Bill of Rights or the First Ten Amendments to the United States Constitution, 68 COM. L.J. 233 (1963) ("I submit that these Ten Amendments are the best answer to those violent, turbulent men of Communistic leanings, both at home and abroad, who would place Might upon the pedestal which others have raised to Right.").

Karl Marx

2. The word "god" probably comes from the Indo-European "ghut" and the old German "guth" giving also the German "gott," the Dutch "god," and Swedish/Danish "gud." JOHN AYTO, DICTIONARY OF WORD ORIGINS 258 (1990). The salutation "goodbye" was originally "God-be-with-you," which Shakespeare rendered "God-be-wy-you" and "God buy' ye." Id. at 259. Interestingly, the word "god" is not related to "good," which instead comes from the prehistoric Germanic "gath" for "bring together," also the source of English's "gather" and "together." Id. at 259.

3. Exodus 20:2–3; see also Deuteronomy 5:6–21.

Exodus (Greek for "departure" and the source of the modern English word "exit"), the second book of the Jewish Torah and Christian Old Testament, tells how Moses led the Israelites out of Egypt. According to Exodus, Moses gave the Israelites the Ten Commandments. Tradition says Moses wrote the five books of the Torah: Genesis, Exodus, Leviticus, Numbers, and Deuteronomy.

4. Exodus 34:15; see also Deuteronomy 5:9; Exodus 20:5.

THE TEN COMMANDMENTS (Paramount Pictures 1956), staring Charlton Heston and Yul Brynner, was Cecil B. DeMille's remake of his 1923 silent film classic THE TEN COMMANDMENTS (Paramount Pictures 1923). Adjusted for inflation, the 1956 version is still the fifth highest grossing movie of all time and is the second highest grossing religious film after Mel Gibson's PASSION OF THE CHRIST (Independent Film 2004). See http://en.wikipedia.org/wiki/The_Ten_Commandments (last visited Sept. 13, 2005).

Cecil B. DeMille

Rather, as the Old Testament's First and Second Commandments show, God helps the Hebrews because they have an exclusive relationship with him:

I am the Lord your God, who brought you out of the land of Egypt, out of the house of slavery; Do not have any other gods before me. [3]

Moses brought forth these commandments from Mount Sinai into a world of competing peoples with their competing gods:

You shall worship no other god, because the Lord, whose name is Jealous, is a jealous God. [4]

So the Bible recognized many deities, but God and the Hebrews were going steady!

Take care not to make a covenant with the inhabitants of the land to which you are going, or it will become a snare among you. You shall tear down their altars, break their pillars, and cut down their sacred poles. [5]

4. *(continued)* The competition of peoples and gods shows in the Golden Calf story, where Moses, upon descending Mount Sinai, destroys the false idol. Also, the special effects centerpiece of THE TEN COMMANDMENTS was the parting of the Red Sea, which was about God beating the Egyptian's gods.

Moses and the Golden Calf by Beccafumi (1537)

5. *Exodus* 34:13–14. Moses set the example and caused quite a stir by descending from Mount Sinai and destroying the original Ten Commandments by hurling them at the golden calf.

Moses with Ten Commandments by Rembrandt (1659)

The Adoration of the Golden Calf by Poussin (1633–34)

Heston backed up by some serious special effects; the "walls" of the Red Sea were made of jello

The Ten Commandments did not allow the Hebrews to "play the field."[1]

As for religion and government, the Hebrews had an early separation of church and state.[2]

God made the judges (and later the kings) separate from the priests.[3] The kings of Israel were not to meddle in the priestly functions.

Once King Saul offered sacrifice to God before a battle because the high priest Samuel was late. When Samuel got there, he rebuked Saul:

"Thou hast done foolishly: thou hast not kept the commandment of the Lord thy God, which he commanded thee: for now would the Lord have established thy kingdom upon Israel forever. But now thy kingdom shall not continue . . . .[4]"

---

1. The Ten Commandments: Still the Center of Controversy!

In *Van Orden v. Perry*, 545 U.S. 677 (2005), the Supreme Court held by a 5–4 vote that the Ten Commandment display at the Texas State Capitol *did not violate* the First Amendment's Establishment Clause. At the same time, however, *McCreary County v. ACLU of Kentucky*, 545 U.S. 844 (2005), held by another 5–4 vote that the Ten Commandment display in a Kentucky courthouse *violated* the Establishment Clause. *See generally* Lael Daniel Weinberger, *The Monument and the Message: Pragmatism and Principle in Establishment Clause Ten Commandments Litigation*, 14 Tex. Wesleyan L. Rev. 393 (2008) ("Public displays of the Ten Commandments have been touchstones of Establishment Clause litigation ever since the Supreme Court ordered a public school to remove a plaque in 1980."); Susanna Dokupil, *"Thou Shalt Not Bear False Witness": "Sham" Secular Purposes in Ten Commandments Displays*, 28 Harv. J.L. & Pub. Pol'y 609, 635 (2005); Thomas B. Colby, *A Constitutional Hierarchy of Religions? Justice Scalia, the Ten Commandments, and the Future of the Establishment Clause*, 100 Nw. U. L. Rev. 1097, 1099–1101 (2006).

According to Justice Stephen Breyer, the "swing vote," the Texas monument had a civic/secular purpose whereas the Kentucky courthouse display was to establish religion. *But see* Douglas Laycock, *Towards a General Theory of the Religion*

Justice Breyer

Heston lays down the law

Cecil B. DeMille

Clauses: The Case of Church Labor Relations and the Right to Church Autonomy, 81 Colum. L. Rev. 1373, 1384 (1981) ("Those who take religion seriously have reason to be alarmed when public officials proclaim that crosses and Christmas carols have no religious significance, or that the Ten Commandments are a secular code.").

But just where did the Texas monument come from? The answer is Cecil B. DeMille. Working through the philanthropic organization, the Fraternal Order of Eagles, he sent hundreds of stone tablet "replicas" to state capitals and court houses just before the release of The Ten Commandments in 1956. ("Replicas" of what?— DeMille did not use one in the movie, and as far as we know, neither God nor Moses spoke the King James Bible's version of English.) But according to Breyer, one of the reasons the Texas monument was acceptable was because it served the very secular (and capitalist) purpose of being a Cecil B. DeMille publicity stunt!

In a dissenting opinion in *Perry*, Justice John Paul Stevens made an important point. How could the DeMille version of the Ten Commandments not establish religion when it presented the specific Protestant King James version? "The Eagles may donate as many monuments as they choose to be displayed in front of Protestant churches,

Ten Commandments monument at the Texas state capitol

benevolent organizations' meeting places, or on the front lawns of private citizens. The expurgated text of the King James version of the Ten Commandments that they have crafted is unlikely to be accepted by Catholic parishes, Jewish synagogues, or even some Protestant denominations, but the message they seek to convey is surely more compatible with church property than with property that is located on the government side of the metaphorical wall."

The books of *Exodus* and *Deuteronomy* give different wordings for the Ten Commandments, thus Jewish, Catholic, various Protestant, and Islamic versions exist.

McCreary County Ten Commandment display

Justice Stevens

So much for Saul trying to gain a little God-power on his own—one word from Samuel, and Saul was out![5]

This was not the only example. When the priests got wind of Judean King Uzziah burning incense to God in the Temple, it was bad news for him:

"And they withstood Uzziah the king, and said unto him, It appertaineth not unto thee, Uzziah, to burn incense unto the Lord, but to the priests the sons of Aaron ... go out of the sanctuary; for thou hast trespassed ....[6]*"*

For overstepping his proper jurisdiction, Uzziah got leprosy.

The Hebrew religious establishment protected its jurisdiction and was clear on what power was separate from the civil government.

---

2. *See generally* Robert Joseph Renaud & Lael Daniel Weinberger, *Spheres of Sovereignty: Church Autonomy Doctrine and the Theological Heritage of the Separation of Church and State*, 35 N. Ky. L. Rev. 67 (2008).

3. *See Exodus* 18:13–26 (regarding the office of judge); *Exodus* 28:1 (regarding the office of priest). Renaud & Weinberger at n.14.

Samuel lays down the law for Saul

4. *1 Samuel* 13:9–14.

6. *2 Chronicles* 26:18; *see also* Renaud & Weinberger at 70–71 (discussing King Jehoshaphat's respect for the separate jurisdictions of the priests and kings, *citing 2 Chronicles* 18:3–6, 19:11).

5. Getting God-power for the army is still in play. Geoffrey R. Stone, *The World of the Framers: A Christian Nation?* 56 UCLA L. Rev. 1, 2–3 (2008), begins his article with but one example from the religious "culture wars." An Air Force Academy graduate objected to the color guard at the Academy lowering the flag to the cross at a ceremony because the oath he took was "to protect and defend the Constitution, not the New Testament."

As for the irony of asking God for the power to kill God's other creations, no one summed it up with bitter irony better than **Abraham Lincoln** in his Second Inaugural Address on March 4, 1865:

™*Both* [sides] *read the same Bible and pray to the same God, and each invokes His aid against the other. It may seem strange that any men should dare to ask a just God's assistance in wringing their bread from the sweat of other men's faces, but let us judge not, that we be not judged. The prayers of both could not be answered. That of neither has been answered fully. The Almighty has His own purposes."*

The Persians:

The first significant instance of what we would recognize as religious tolerance was in the Persian Empire under Cyrus the Great.

In contrast to the Hebrews tearing down their neighbor's altars, Cyrus proclaimed that he

"repaired the ruined temples in the cities he conquered, restored their cults, and returned their sacred images . . . ."[1]

Even the Hebrews praised Cyrus's tolerance in allowing them to return to Jerusalem and rebuild the Temple:

"In the first year of King Cyrus, Cyrus the king issued a decree: Concerning the house of God at Jerusalem let the temple . . . be rebuilt . . . . And let the cost be paid from the royal treasury. Also let the gold and silver utensils . . . be returned and brought to their places in the temple in Jerusalem; and you shall put them in the house of God."[2]

Cyrus' proclamation went beyond toleration in that he publicly worshiped the

---

1. Cyrus's proclamation is on the **Cyrus Cylinder**, found in 1879 in modern-day Iran. Cyrus issued it in cuneiform script circa 539 BC, after he conquered Babylon.

See generally Hirad Abtahi, *Reflections on the Ambiguous Universality of Human Rights: Cyrus the Great's Proclamation as a Challenge to the Athenian Democracy's Perceived Monopoly on Human Rights*, 36 Denv. J. Int'l L. & Pol'y 55, 58–59 (2007) (arguing that Cyrus's proclamation recognized that nature gives individuals human rights that thus limits the ruler's power).

2. *Ezra 6:3–5.* The full quote shows the specificity of Cyrus's decree:
"In the first year of King Cyrus, Cyrus the king issued a decree: Concerning the house of God at Jerusalem, let the temple, the place where sacrifices are offered, be rebuilt and let its foundations be retained, its height being 60 cubits and its width 60 cubits; with three layers of huge stones and one layer of timbers. And let the cost be paid from the royal treasury. Also let the gold and silver utensils of the house of God, which Nebuchadnezzar took from the temple in Jerusalem and brought to Babylon, be returned and brought to their places in the temple in Jerusalem; and you shall put them in the house of God."

See also *Ezra 1:1–11; Isaiah 45:1–6* (praising Cyrus's humanity and justice).

Medieval painting showing Cyrus the Great allowing the Hebrews to return to Jerusalem and the Temple's rebuilding (1470)

gods of the peoples whom he vanquished, such as the Babylonian god Marduk:

"[Cyrus] sought to worship him each day . . . . Cyrus, the king, his worshipper . . . May all the gods . . . say to Marduk, my lord that Cyrus, the king who worships you . . . ."[3]

Certainly Cyrus made a good public relations move with this one! But it went beyond a mere PR stunt to show something else about rights and religion.

It was not the king and his god that subjected and ruled over people, or even the king/god of the Egyptians.[4] Instead, Cyrus' dynasty worshipped Ahura-Mazda.[5]

Unlike most ancient gods, Ahura-Mazda is a moral and spiritual essence rather than a material or natural force. Ahura-Mazda was preoccupied with the reign of justice and a struggle where the forces of light (justice) confront the forces of darkness (injustice) through law.[6]

3. *Quoted in* Abtahi at 66.

4. For much of Egyptian history, the pharaohs claimed to be incarnations of the god Horus.

5. Abtahi at 62.

Horus

Horus and Seth crowning Ramses III

Ahura-Mazda   Marduk

6. Abtahi at 62 (discussing how the Persians incorporated the beliefs of the ancient Iranian prophet and religious poet Zoroaster (Zarathustra) regarding the struggle of light and dark; good and evil). Zoroaster influenced the Greeks and Europe to the extent that Raphael included him in his painting *The School of Athens* (1509).

Detail of Zoroaster and a star-studded globe

Scene from the Persian capital, Persepolis, showing the dark god Angra Mainyu killing the primeval bull and temporarily taking the universe out of balance

In this cosmology, the king has the moral imperative to effect justice. Though maybe ethereal, it is objective; that is, outside the king. The king no longer rules just in his own interest but bows before a broader concept.

Cyrus, then, may have given the world its first separation between the secular (the king and positive law) and the spiritual (Ahura-Mazda and justice) spheres.[1] Or, as Thomas Jefferson would later say, a "*Separation of Church and State.*"

Taken to its fullest extent,

Cyrus and his notion of justice beyond the human realm would be the basis of natural law and even the premise of the DECLARATION OF INDEPENDENCE that

"We hold these truths to be self-evident that all men are created equal . . . ."[2]

The Hebrews were not the only ones who admired Cyrus. The Greeks were also fans; remarkable because they often warred against the Persian Empire.[3]

Plato recognized the balance the Persians created

between slavery and freedom. When the Persians shared freedom with their subjects, government worked better because

"soldiers were friendly to their officers [and] wise men free to give counsel."[4]

The Persians, following Cyrus's lead, also allowed free speech because

"the king was not jealous but allowed free speech and respected those who could help at all by their counsel, such a man had the opportunity of contributing to

---

1. Abtahi at 66, arguing that "[b]y referring to a reality beyond human reality, which constitutes humans' last resort to defend their rights against authoritarianism, Cyrus refers to what would be called natural law . . . ."

2. THE DECLARATION OF INDEPENDENCE, para. 2 (U.S. 1976).
See Abtahi at 66–67, arguing that Cyrus and his proclamation may have prefigured Article 18 of the UNIVERSAL DECLARATION OF HUMAN RIGHTS that
"[e]veryone has the right to freedom of thought, conscience and religion; this right includes freedom to change his religion or belief, and freedom, either alone or in community with others and in public or private, to manifest his religion or belief in teaching, practice, worship and observance."
UNIVERSAL DECLARATION OF HUMAN RIGHTS, G.A. Res. 217A, at 71, U.N. GAOR, 3d Sess., 1st plen. mtg., U.N. Doc A/810 (Dec. 10, 1948), *quoted in* Abtahi at 66–67.

3. Probable relief of Persian King Xerxes, who launched the invasion of Greece in 480 BC.

Eleanor Roosevelt holds a Spanish version of the Universal Declaration of Human Rights

4. Abtahi at 83 (discussing Plato's *Laws*). This, of course, is not the Hollywood image of Persians from the "sandal epic" THE 300 SPARTANS (20th Century Fox 1962) to the fanciful but visually stunning 300 (WARNER BROTHERS 2007).

5. Abtahi at 83. Abtahi goes on to note that Plato develops the idea of a society based on the mutual exchange of reason as the bases of a *res publica* (citing PLATO, THE REPUBLIC (trans. Benjamin Jowett 2009), *available at* http://classics.mit.edu/Plato/republic.html). Later in this chapter, compare Sir Thomas More's PETITION FOR FREE SPEECH in Parliament.

the common stock the fruit of his wisdom."

Because of free speech, men of ability rose in the empire and

"all their affairs made progress, owing to their freedom, friendliness and mutual exchange of reason." [5]

Speaking of The Greeks:

The Greeks prized this free mutual exchange of reason, at least in the abstract. The first historian, Herodotus, who wrote about the Persian War, noted that freedom and free speech were good for government:

"And it is plain enough, not from this instance only, but from many everywhere, that freedom is an excellent thing."

Indeed, because of the freedom to speak the Athenians had become fierce fighters:

"Even the Athenians, who, while they continued under the rule of tyrants, were not a whit more valiant than any of their neighbors, no sooner shook off

the yoke than they became decidedly the first of all."* [6]

Herodotus explains the psychology of freedom:

"These things show that, while undergoing oppression, they let themselves be beaten, since then they worked for a master; but so soon as they got their freedom, each man was eager to do the best he could for himself." [7]

Herodotus's contemporary and successor in the western historical tradition, Thucydides, picked up on the same theme of connecting freedom and government:

---

6. See online text and translation at http://www.sacred-texts.com/cla/hh/hh5070.htm (last visited July 14, 2009).

Herodotus

Fourth century BC Athenian warrior leaving for war

7. Writing about a war 2,500 years after the Persian Wars, historian Stephen Ambrose quotes General Maxwell Taylor about the 101st Airborne Division during World War II: *"The men were hardened, the officers tested, their equipment upgraded and they had that wonderful flexibility and self-confidence imparted by a democratic society. No other system could produce soldiers like that."* STEPHEN E. AMBROSE, D-DAY JUNE 6, 1944: THE CLIMACTIC BATTLE OF WORLD WAR II 53 (1994). As Ambrose later analyzed in STEPHEN E. AMBROSE, THE VICTORS: EISENHOWER AND HIS BOYS: THE MEN OF WORLD WAR II 183–84 (1998), *"[t]he men fighting for democracy were able to make quick, on-site decisions and act on them; the men fighting for the totalitarian regime were not. Except for a captain here, a lieutenant there, not one German officer reacted appropriately to the challenge of D-Day."*

General Dwight D. Eisenhower visits the 101st Airborne before D-Day and Athenians before battle

Gen. Taylor

"Here [in Athens] each individual is interested not only in his own affairs but in the affairs of the state as well . . . . Of all people we alone do not say that a man who takes no interest in politics is a man who minds his own business, but we say that he is useless."

With respect to speech,

Thucydides specifically noted that

"the worst thing is to rush into action before the consequences have been properly debated."[1]

The Athenians, then, invented our notion of freedom of speech. Any citizen could address the assembly, the courts, or the

government and also could move legislation.[2]

Thucydides contrasts Athens with its rival, Sparta, showing that the Greek world was not unanimous regarding ideas of civil freedom and speech, and this underlay the conflict between the two Greek states.

Indeed, in terminology

Pericles

Brandeis

1. THUCYDIDES, THE PELOPONNESIAN WAR, *quoted in* WILTSHIRE at 113.

Thucydides is quoting the funeral speech of Pericles. Over two millennia later, Justice Louis Brandeis echoed that *"the greatest menace to freedom is an inert people."* Whitney v. California, 274 U.S. 357, 375 (1927) (Brandeis, J., concurring). Following Herodotus, Pericles notes the relationship between freedom and courage:

™*[H]appiness . . . [is] the fruit of freedom and freedom of valor . . . ."*

Quoted in Keith Werhan, *The Classical Athenian Ancestry of American Freedom of Speech,* 2008 SUP. CT. REV. 293, 310. Brandeis again picked up the theme: *"liberty . . . [is] the secret of happiness and courage [is] the secret of liberty."* Whitney at 375.

2. WILTSHIRE at 114–15. The Athenians called this *"isēgoria"* ("the equal right to speak") for everyone who wished to address the boule, ecclesia, or jury courts. WILTSHIRE at 112; Werhan at 300. *"[I]sēgoria"* is synonymous with democracy. *See* WILTSHIRE at 119 and 123 (*"[i]sēgoria"* was part of the freedom of assembly).

The ideal assembly speaker (*"rhētōr"*) was an "honest, ordinary citizen" who spoke simply and truthfully when he occasionally ascended the speaker's platform. Werhan at 303. This is the American ideal as well. In Norman Rockwell's *Save Freedom of Speech,* a man in a workshirt, with calloused hands, stands to voice an opinion at a town meeting, while

others, including men in suits and ties, look on. The *Saturday Evening Post* published this color lithograph in 1942 as part of the "Four Freedoms" series to encourage Americans to buy war bonds during World War II. Again, the image evokes Herodotus's and Thucydides's description of a democracy at war: *"so soon as they got their freedom, each man was eager to do the best he could for himself."*

The Greek world at the time of the conflict between Athens and Sparta

that reflects a modern free speech debate, the Athenian Demosthenes noted the role of speech in a free society rather than in a closed one:

"The fundamental difference between the Athenian and the Spartan constitutions is that in Athens you are free to praise the Spartan consti-tution, whereas in Sparta you are not allowed to praise any constitution other than the Spartan." [3]

So a very modern free speech debate played out in the ancient Greek world, with Athenian Greeks extolling the value of free speech and Spartan Greeks extolling the virtues of security. This language parallels the Cold War between the United States and the old Soviet Union about the nature of freedom and society.[4]

But just as America did not always stay true to its free speech foundation during the Cold War,[5] Athens did not always stay true to its own innovations of democracy and free speech.

3. *Quoted in* WILTSHIRE at 113.

4. Kruschev meeting with Kennedy during the Cold War. *See* Werhan at 313.

In *Debs v. United States*, 249 U.S. 211 (1919), the Supreme Court upheld his conviction. Debs eventually got a presidential pardon.

Election poster for Debs, Socialist Party of America candidate for president in 1904

In *Schenck v. United States*, 249 U.S. 47 (1919), the Supreme Court upheld the conviction of a person for circulating leaflets that argued that conscription is involuntary servitude. *Whitney v. California*, 274 U.S. 357 (1927), *overruled by Brandenburg v. Ohio*, 395 U.S. 444 (1969), upheld the conviction of an individual under the California Criminal Syndicalism Act for attending a Communist Labor Party convention. In *Dennis v. United States,* 341 U.S. 494 (1951), the Supreme Court upheld the convictions of the Communist Party leaders for advocating Marxist-Leninist ideology. Again, America has not always lived up to its free speech ideal.

5. Communism Cases. America has a history of trying to restrict communist speech.

Congress passed the Espionage Act of 1917 to target communists. O'Brien at 47. Presidential candidate and labor leader Eugene V. Debs was convicted and imprisoned under it for speaking against American involvement in World War I.

Eugene V. Debs

Debs in a federal penitentiary

World War I poster

In 399 BC, the Athenians put the philosopher Socrates on trial, not for anything he did but for what he said.

What we know of Socrates's trial comes from his student, Plato. In the *Euthyphro, Apology, Crito,* and *Phaedo*, Plato made Socrates's trial the central theme.[1] Socrates faced trumped up charges of "*corrupting the youth*" and "*disbelieving in the ancestral gods,*" showing once again the thematic connection between speech and religion. Plato's point is that speaking truth often offends the dogmatic.[2]

And for speaking the truth, the Athenians tried, convicted, and had Socrates kill himself with hemlock.[3] Even in Athens, the cradle of free speech, the right to speak and believe without government restriction was fragile.

---

1. See **Chapter 7 of** *Bills, Quills, and Stills*, (**Constitution Press re-release 2017**) for a brief discussion of the Socrates trial in the context of the history of juries.

"COME UNTO ME, YE OPPREST!"
—Alley in the Memphis *Commercial Appeal.*

Political cartoon of the era depicting an anarchist attempting to destroy the Statue of Liberty

Senator Joseph McCarthy chats with Roy Cohn at the McCarthy Hearings

2. "*Humans,*" said Socrates, "*do not know anything worthwhile.*" He believed the human condition does not allow certainty of moral truth and therefore we never know for sure whether our belief regarding "truth" is correct. Werhan at 326, *quoting* Plato's *Apology*. For Socrates, only a god could possess true wisdom.

Socrates

3. For the effect of hemlock on the body, see **Chapter 8 of** *Bills, Quills, and Stills*, (**Constitution Press re-release 2017**).

The Death of Socrates by David (1787)

The Romans:

Romans of the republic and the early empire lived in one of history's most class-conscious societies. Not every citizen was free to speak, and Romans did not share the notion of freedom of assembly.[4]

They instead divided government along ideas of separating power among the classes: the monarchy (consuls), aristocracy (senators), and the democracy (people).[5] Only members of the senatorial class, the patricians, were supposed to speak their mind on politics, leaving normal citizens, the plebians, with only a representative voice in the office of the Tribune of the Plebs (*tribuni plebis*).

The Romans feared popular power and created an entire constitutional structure to hinder it. Ironically, all the constraints led to a government that lacked the ability to prevent that most popular of Romans, Julius Caesar, from usurping the whole thing.[6]

4. WILTSHIRE at 116.

5. WILTSHIRE at 127. This formed the precursor of the U.S. Constitution's separation of powers among the executive, legislative, and judicial branches of government.

The Supreme Court building of the judicial branch

The Capitol dome of the legislative branch

6. WILTSHIRE at 129. In 49 BC, Julius Caesar crossed the Rubicon River to march on Rome. This was the boundary that a Roman general could not cross while still commanding troops. By so doing, Caesar was in rebellion against the Roman Republic. Thus the term "crossing the Rubicon" has come to mean passing a point of no return.

The White House—Presidential residence of the executive branch

But even the senators were not wholly free to speak their minds. The Romans had two elected "censors" (*censura*) to supervise counting the Roman population and to guard the "public morality" (*regimen morum*).[1] This is where we get our modern words "census," "censor," and "censorship."[2]

Defending public morality was a full-time job in the late Roman republic.[3] Censors did not just have to prevent crime and "immorality," they also had to maintain the traditional Roman character, ethics, and habits (*mos majorum*).[4]

But the job came with a lot of power. Because the censors controlled the census, they could expel a person from the list of Roman citizens and, thus, expel a senator from the Senate.

1. The census determined the senate list (*lectio senatus*) and the equatorial rank (*recognitio equitum*). Censors administered public buildings and the building of new public works.

U.S. Const. Art. I, § 2, provides that the government must conduct a census every ten years. In modern America, census counters use handheld computers, and the count influences the distribution of public money and building projects, an interesting tie to the old Roman job of censor.

2. This dour fellow is **Cato the Elder**, censor of Rome in 184 B.C., who was just the man to ferret out immorality! The word "*censor*" comes from the Latin "*senex*" ("old") and is also the root for "senator," "senior," and "senile." Ayto at 467.

3. *Romans in the Decadence of the Empire* by Couture (1847). ↓

4. Activities that could get you in trouble with the censors included the following:

- living in celibacy when you ought to be providing new citizens;
- improperly dissolving a marriage or engagement;
- improperly treating your wife, children, or parents;
- spending money extravagantly;
- neglecting your fields;
- being cruel toward slaves or clients;
- having a disreputable occupation like acting;
- defrauding orphans.

Additionally, the censors policed public officials for malfeasance in office and perjury. But because it took two censors to act, a politician needed only to bribe one to get virtual immunity.

5. The censors are the origin of the modern "censure." The U.S. Senate and House still "censure" people, but it is only a public reprimand without legal consequence. In fact, it has no basis in the Constitution or Senate and House rules. On December 2, 1954, the Senate censured Republican Senator McCarthy for failing to cooperate with and insulting the subcommittee investigating him. Lewis at 123. "McCarthyism" ebbed with McCarthy's disgrace and death.

Joseph McCarthy

Because of this, censors were also known as *castigatores* ("chastisers").[5]

The censor could be useful to Roman politicians. The trick was to show your political enemy's immorality in a way that would trigger the censors' power of negating his citizenship, and thus his political voice. Indeed, public morality could easily expand to include what a person said rather than what he did.

The Roman censorship lasted from 443 to 22 BC, a total of 421 years. The office, in fact, did not really end. Emperors saw the value of having the power of censorship and thus took on the office under the title *praefectura morum* ("prefect of the morals").[6] Popes picked it up from there.[7]

6. Caesar Augustus, the first Roman emperor, took the censor job in 28 B.C.

The emperor also took over the job of *pontifex maximus*, heading the Ancient Roman College of Pontiffs and thus all religious institutions.

™*Pontifex* means "bridge builder" ("*pons*" + "*facere*") and "*maximus*" means "greatest," as in the English "maximum." Originally, a "pontiff" probably built Roman bridges over the Tiber, a sacred river and deity. Thus, symbolically "pontiff" meant one who could bridge the divide between gods and men. In this sense, beginning perhaps as early as the late fourth century, the popes took on the title. *See* Encyclopedia of Catholicism 1010 (Richard P. McBrien ed.,1995).

7. The early Roman emperors took on the title *primus inter pares* ("first among equals") to reduce the appearance of a dictatorship.

In Christianity, the Eastern Orthodox Churches recognized the pope as *primus inter pares,* but Rome stayed with the idea of papal supremacy.

"First among equals" also describes the Chief Justice of the United States, who, despite having considerable administrative powers, has no direct control over the other justices' decisions.

The Roberts Court in 2009

Ancient Roman bridge over the Tiber

Emperor Augustus in the robes of *pontifex maximus*

Pope Benedict XIV as *pontifex maximus*

Chief Justice John Roberts

Despite the Roman obsession with public morality, they were both tolerant and practical regarding religion, especially with respect to maintaining the power of the state.

As the Roman statesman Cicero noted,

> *"Jupiter is called Best and Greatest not because he makes us just or sober or wise but safe and secure, rich and prosperous."*[1]

Roman religion, like the Old Testament Hebrew religion, centered on success.

For the Romans, more gods meant more success.[2] Incorporation was the policy; they simply added a newly conquered people's local gods to the Roman pantheon and often gave them Roman names. And as long as a religion was willing to give the emperor his due,[3] its adherents were free to practice as they pleased.

And so things went with the Romans, at least until somewhere around the year 30 AD, when they executed an obscure teacher (rabbi), challenging an obscure faith, from one of the empire's many backwater provinces. This rabbi's followers would create a religion that ended up taking over the Empire.

The rabbi was Jesus.

---

1. WILTSHIRE at 105, *quoting* CICERO, DE NATURA DEORUM 3.36). "By Jove!"—Jupiter was the Roman version of the Greek Zeus. The names Jupiter, Jove, and Zeus all have a common Indo-European root that includes the Latin *"dues,"* which translates into English as "God" and is the source of the English word "deity." *See* WEBSTER'S NEW INTERNATIONAL DICTIONARY OF THE ENGLISH LANGUAGE 691 (2d ed. 1942). The planet Jupiter is named for the Roman god.

Jupiter and Thétis by Ingres (1811)

2. WILTSHIRE at 104–05.

3. The empire brought a new fusion of state and religion with the "divine" emperor. WILTSHIRE at 106. For the Romans, it was not so much that the emperor himself was a god (unlike the Egyptian pharaohs) but that the emperor personified Rome's divine authority.

Christ the Savior, a sixth century icon from Saint Catherine's Monastery, Mount Sinai

4. Jesus (c. 4 BC–c. 30 AD), also known as Jesus Christ or Jesus the Christ, is Christianity's central figure, and most Christian denominations venerate him as the son of God and God incarnate. Christians also believe he is the messiah (savior) that the Old Testament foretold. Judaism rejects these claims, and Islam considers Jesus a prophet.

"Christ" is English for the Greek *"Khristós"* ("the anointed") a translation of the Hebrew ("*Mašía*" or "mashiach," which also means "messiah"), as in someone God has anointed for a special mission. The English spelling "Christ" comes from the seventeenth century, with Old and Middle English usually spelling it "Crist," with a short *i*, preserved in the modern pronunciation of "Christmas."

5. "Christ!," "Jesus!," or "Jesus Christ!" are interjections or exclamations often used in surprise or anger, and they are not usually direct religious references. Some Christians believe they violate the Third Commandment against taking the Lord's name in vain and are thus blasphemous. To avoid the rebuke of "using the Lord's name in vain," circumlocutions and euphemisms exist, such as starting with "Jesus" and quickly adding "Mary and Joseph!" to make it sound like a religious invocation rather than like a curse.

WWJD—WHAT WOULD JESUS DO— UNDER THE FIRST AMENDMENT?

Jesus did nothing; at least not anything that should have gotten the Romans to execute him.[4]

He committed no crime of which we know.[5] He did not lead armed revolutionaries. He conspired to commit no illegal deed.

Perhaps he blasphemed against the Hebrews' idea of God, but what would the Romans have cared about that?[5] Besides, the punishment for a blasphemer or a heretic was stoning, not crucifixion.[6] So what stake did the Romans have in the Hebrews' theological argument with the son of a carpenter?[7]

The answer is the power of speech and religion.

They killed Jesus for what he said.[8]

Jesus, through religious speech, challenged the powerful. For that they killed him:

> *"Then the whole assembly rose and led him off to Pilate. And they began to accuse him, saying, 'We have found this man subverting our nation. He opposes payment of taxes to Caesar and claims to be Christ/Messiah, a king.'"*[9]

6. Indeed, the Romans specifically killed Jesus with crucifixion—the best audio-visual aid in the ancient world for making a political point. See **Chapter 8 of Bills, Quills, and Stills, (Constitution Press re-release 2017).**

A Byzantine crucifixion icon, Athens, Greece. An icon is a depiction of Christian religious art. It is not painted but "written," again showing the connection between speech and religion.

8. *Sermon on the Mount* by Bloch.

7. Historians generally accept that a man named Jesus lived, giving at least some credibility to the Bible as an historical source. Additionally, the Jewish historian Flavius Josephus wrote in 93 or 94 AD in his *Antiquities of the Jews* that

> ™[n]ow there was about this time Jesus, a wise man, if it be lawful to call him a man; for he was a doer of wonderful works, a teacher of such men as receive the truth with pleasure. He drew over to him both many of the Jews and many of the Gentiles. He was Christ. And when Pilate, at the suggestion of the principal men amongst us, had condemned him to the cross, those that loved him at the first did not forsake him; for he appeared to them alive again the third day, as the divine prophets had foretold these and ten thousand other wonderful things concerning him. And the tribes of Christians, so named from him, are not extinct at this day."

THE WORKS OF FLAVIUS JOSPEHUS 612 (William Whiston trans., 1847).

9. *Luke 23:1–4.*

The Tribute Money by Masaccio

Accusing Jesus of opposing taxes was a ploy to get the Romans to kill him. Jesus's opponents had asked him whether they should pay Roman taxes. He famously asked for a Roman coin and responded that they should

"[g]ive to Caesar what is Caesar's, and to God what is God's."[1]

In this statement, Jesus himself laid the ground-work for the separation of church and state. During his trial, Jesus expanded the theme when responding to Pontius Pilate, the provincial governor and his prosecutor:

"My kingdom is not of this world. If my kingdom were of this world, my servants would have been fighting, that I might not be deliv-ered over to the Jews."[2]

But many Christians, both then and now, did not see this as a prescription to separate church and state.[3] Rather they saw it as delin-eating a Christian's role in the church-state struggle:

---

1. *Matthew* 22:21.

2. *John* 18:36. Jesus' trial before the Roman Pontius Pilate is a key part of the drama or "pas-sion." Pilate usually comes across as sympathetic to Jesus; after all, Rome later became one of Christianity's centers. For Jesus' trial in film see e.g.,

THE LAST TEMPTATION OF CHRIST (Universal Studios 1988)

THE PASSION OF THE CHRIST (Newmarket Films 2004)

MONTY PYTHON'S LIFE OF BRIAN (Warner Brothers 1979)

JESUS CHRIST SUPERSTAR (Universal Studios 1973)

3. Christians recognize the duty from the Old Testament to acknowl-edge God:

> ™*Be wise now therefore, O ye kings: be in-structed, ye judges of the earth. Serve the Lord with fear, and rejoice with trembling. Kiss the Son . . . ."*

Psalms 2:10–11, discussed in Weinberger at 410, citing 1 JOHN CALVIN, COMMENTARY ON THE BOOK OF PSALMS 22–27 (James Anderson trans., 1845; photo. reprint 2005) (commenting on the Protestant view of the individual's duty of acknowledgement); Pope Leo XIII, *The Christian Constitution of States*, Encyclical Letter Immortale Dei, Nov. 1, 1885, *in* JOHN A. RYAN & MOORHOUSE F.X. MILLAR, THE STATE AND THE CHURCH 1, 2–4 (1924), *available at* http:// www.ewtn. com/library/encyc/ l13sta.htm (stating the Catholic view of the individual's duty of acknowledgement).

Christ before Pilate (1881)

"We ought to obey God rather than men." [4]

This creed led many to the arena.

CHRISTIANS AND LIONS

Christians got into trouble because they would not give the emperor his due.

For the Romans, *pieta* ("piety") in religion was supposed to promote unity and loyalty to Rome; not the point of Christianity. Because the Roman view of religion was utilitarian, they believed bad things would happen if people did not properly respect the gods. After all, these traditional "pagan" gods had treated Rome pretty well, so why mess with success! [5]

This is where "throwing Christians to the lions in the arena" came about. [6] Generally, persecution of Christians was sporadic and not necessarily government policy. But some emperors did implement a broader persecution policy. The first and most famous was Nero. [7]

---

4. *Acts of the Apostles*

5. The Roman Empire in 117 AD, at its greatest extent.

6. *The Christian Martyrs' Last Prayer* by Gerome (1883).

7. Nero (37–68 AD) needed political cover in 64 AD, when Rome caught fire and he got blamed. In response, Nero blamed the Christians; after all, they did not honor the gods. Following a long artistic tradition of presenting Nero in a bad light, Hollywood took a shot in Quo Vadis (MGM 1951), where Peter Ustinov gave the definitive Nero. *"Quo vadis"* is Latin for *"Where are you going?"* It refers to the story that Christ met Saint Peter on the Appian Way, fleeing Nero's persecution. Peter asked Christ, *"Domine, quo vadis?"* (*"Lord, where are you going?"*) and Christ answered *"Eo Romam iterum crucifigi."* (*"I am going to Rome to be crucified again."*). Peter took this to mean that he had to return to Rome to be crucified, so that Christ would not have to be crucified again. They crucified Saint Peter at the foot of Vatican Hill on the current site of Saint Peter's Basilica.

Crucifixion of Saint Peter by Caravaggio. Saint Peter asked to be crucified upside down so as not to be compared to Jesus.

Peter Ustinov as Nero

A Christian Dirce by Siemiradzki. Nero (center) looks on at a martyred Christian woman.

Church of Domine Quo Vadis, where Peter met Christ

Saint Peter's Basilica from the Tiber River

CONSTANTINE TO THE RESCUE

At least so Constantine said!

The traditional view is that Constantine embraced Christianity after God gave him a vision before the Battle of Milvian Bridge in 312 AD. Looking up, Constantine saw a cross of light and the words,

"Ev Toutw Nika" (or, in Latin, "in hoc signo vinces"; in English, "by this sign, conquer.")[1]

He had his troops, so the story goes, paint their shields with the Christian Chi Ro symbol.[2] Constantine won the battle and ended up emperor; otherwise we would not talk about him today.

From this point on, Rome tolerated Christianity throughout the empire.[3] For this, Constantine is known as the first Christian Roman emperor and was made a saint.[4]

But leaving aside Constantine's personal religiosity, his flirtation with the Christians paid off politically. If he had stayed with the old pagan faiths, the most he would

1. *Constantine's Conversion* by Rubens, showing him before the Battle of Milvian Bridge.

A coin of Constantine (c. 337 AD) showing the Chi Rho on the Roman standard (*labarum*) spearing a serpent

2. *Constantine the Great,* THE CATHOLIC ENCYCLOPEDIA, http://www. newadvent. org/ cathen/04295c. htm (last visited Aug. 2, 2009).

The Chi Rho is a very early Christian symbol made by superimposing the first two Greek letters of "Christ" ("Χριστός"); *chi* equals *ch* and *rho* equals *r*, to produce the monogram ☧. Though not technically a cross, the Chi Rho invokes Jesus's crucifixion.

3. As the story goes, his mother, Saint Helena, prayed and prayed for him to accept Christianity. She then went to the Holy Land and found the True Cross. *St. Helena,* THE CATHOLIC ENCYCLOPEDIA, http://www. newadvent. org/cathen/07202b.htm (last visited Aug. 2, 2009). The fact that she found it over 300 years after the crucifixion adds to the miraculous nature of the discovery. Of course, there were so many pieces of the "true cross" in Europe's churches that they would make a forest of crosses.

4. Not bad, given that he did not convert until his deathbed. The last-minute absolution must have been a good precaution. After all, during his reign he killed a number of rivals and courtiers. He also killed his wife Fausta by locking her in an overheated bath and his oldest son Cripus by poisoning him.

Helena and the true cross in Saint Peter's Bascilica

Helena of Constantinople, mother of Constantine I, 325–26 AD

The Baptism of Constantine by students of Raphael

have gotten would have been to be a "divine" emperor and the *pontifex maximus* ("chief of the pagan priests"). Roman history showed that neither title protected an emperor from assassination.

With Christianity, though, he got to be God's hand-picked savior, chosen under the sign of the cross at Milvian Bridge to kill everyone else.[5] And at the time, Christianity was a mess! In fact, it really was not Christianity but *Christianities* floating around the Roman world.[6] The "church" could not even agree on a basic creed or statement of belief.

Thus Constantine got to be God's broker— politically *way* better than being a dusty old "divine" emperor![7]

It was Constantine, not the bishops, who called the "church" to Nicaea (in modern Turkey) in 325 AD to have the bishops come up with the first truly universal statement of Christian belief.[8] This became known as the Nicene Creed, which most major Christian denominations use in some form even today.[9]

5. Constantine's colossal head. He is not portrayed as divine but chosen, with his gaze looking up to God. Overall, it gives the message that this is a guy you do not want to mess with!

6. Arianism was one of the Christianities. Bishop Arius from Alexandria, Egypt, in the early 300s denied that Jesus was fully God. Rather, the Father, in the beginning, created (or begot) the Son, and the Son, with the Father, created the world. This made the Son (Jesus) just a created being and not God. Regarding Arian Christianity, *see Arianism*, THE CATHOLIC ENCYCLOPEDIA, http://www.newadvent.org/cathen/01707c.htm (last visited June 12, 2009).

7. In fact, he got to be "Constantine the Great" and even Saint Constantine, as this mosaic centuries later shows. Hagia Sophia, Constantinople (Istanbul), c. 1000.

8. Constantine (center) and the Fathers of the First Council of Nicaea (325) holding the Nicene Creed in its 381 form.

9. The Modern Nicene Creed.
™*We believe in one God, the Father, the Almighty, maker of heaven and earth, of all that is, seen and unseen.*
We believe in one Lord, Jesus Christ, the only son of God, eternally begotten of the Father, God from God, Light from Light, true God from true God, begotten, not made, of one being with the Father.
Through him all things were made.
For us and for our salvation he came down from heaven: by the power of the Holy Spirit he became incarnate from the Virgin Mary, and was made man.
For our sake he was crucified under Pontius Pilate; he suffered death and was buried.
On the third day he rose again in accordance with the Scriptures; he ascended into heaven and is seated at the right hand of the Father.
He will come again in glory to judge the living and the dead,
and his kingdom will have no end.
We believe in the Holy Spirit, the Lord, the giver of life, who proceeds from the Father [and the Son].
With the Father and the Son he is worshipped and glorified.
He has spoken through the Prophets.
We believe in one holy catholic and apostolic Church.
We acknowledge one baptism for the forgiveness of sins.
We look for the resurrection of the dead, and the life of the world to come. Amen."

Despite becoming a saint, Constantine could be perfectly pagan when it suited his political need. His arch of triumph in Rome makes no mention of Christ and uses no Christian symbols.[1] In his mix of Christianity, paganism, and state power, Constantine had the best of it all. Forget any separation of church and state; for Constantine it was his two "churches," Christian and pagan, that served the state, that is, him.[2]

Constantine would not have understood our modern concept of "the state." Rather, during this age it was the city, the Greek concept of the *polis*, that mattered. After all, it was the Roman Empire he ruled, named after the city of Rome. Even the later Byzantine Empire was named after Byzantium, Constantinople's old name before Constantine moved in.[3]

Constantine and his successors ruled for centuries over this "city" of Byzantium.[4] But it would take a Christian bishop and former pagan to define the place of something that was more than just the emperor's "city of men." There was something separate, which in many ways was a foundation for the later concept of separation of church and state.

This separate "place" is Saint Augustine of Hippo's CITY OF GOD.

1. The Arch of Constantine (315) in Rome commemorates Constantine's victory at Milvian bridge in 312. The fact that the Arch has no Christian symbols could be because the builders stole the art from older Roman buildings and monuments in a technique called "spolia."

2. Constantine the Great crowned by Constantinople. It is the city, personified as a goddess, which crowns him, not a pagan priest or Christian bishop. Even in his symbols, Constantine would cede no power to the church. As we will see, this is the type of power and status that Henry VIII of England lusted after.

3. In 1453 the Ottoman Turks took the city, renamed it Istanbul, and ended the Byzantine Empire for good. But you can still see the old Byzantine parts and ruins today, as featured in the James Bond movie FROM RUSSIA WITH LOVE (United Artists 1963).

4. At the risk of getting ahead of the story, **John Milton**, the author of PARADISE LOST, also wrote that Constantine was Christianity's worst corrupter. *See* John Witte, Jr., *Prophets, Priests, and Kings: John Milton and the Reformation of Rights and Liberties in England*, 57 EMORY L.J. 1527, 1562 (2008). For Milton, the early church had faithfully lived by *"rendering unto Caesar what was Caesar's"* and leaving God the rest. Despite persecutions, the church thrived for three centuries. Then Constantine came along and took *"things that were God's."* Constantine sponsored the church, called the church councils, controlled church property, and appointed the bishops. For Milton, Protestants and Catholics alike had been *"enthralled"* and *"seduced"* by Constantine's (i.e., the state's) *"lavish superstition"* that church and state needed each other. According to Milton, Christians *"should not suffer the two powers, the ecclesiastical and the civil, which are so totally distinct, to commit whoredom together."* *Id.* at 1562.

5. Botticelli's *Augustine* is a nice-looking Italian man at his desk. But given that Augustine was a Berber from North Africa, the older portrait is closer to the mark; Augustine was probably black. On Augustine generally, *see* PETER BROWN, AUGUSTINE OF HIPPO (1967); GARRY WILLS, SAINT AUGUSTINE (1999); *Saint Augustine*, THE CATHOLIC ENCYCLOPEDIA, http://www.newadvent.org/fathers/1201.htm (last visited Aug. 6, 2009).

Augustine by Sandro Botticelli (c. 1480)

Early sixth century portrait of Augustine

SEPARATING CHURCH AND STATE IN *THE CITY OF GOD*

Saint Augustine wrote THE CITY OF GOD (*De Civitate Dei*, also known as *De Civitate Dei contra Paganos* or *The City of God against the Pagans*) in the early fifth century.[5] The book is about God, martyrdom, Jews, and Christianity's relationship with competing religions and philosophies.

Augustine wrote it just after the Visigoths sacked Rome in 410 AD.[6] The Roman Empire, the "city of man," was failing. Augustine offered the "city of God" as consolation.

Even though Christianity was the empire's official religion, Augustine clarified that its message was essentially spiritual, not political. Human history was a conflict between the cities of God and man.[7]

In the city of God, people forgo earthly pleasure for Christian values. Conversely, the city of Man is always divided against itself, and the strong oppress the weak for their own interests and lusts. All of this was not supposed to happen in the church, the city of God on earth.

Despite Augustine, the centuries would show that it was hard to maintain the separation, especially when the church became the only real government in Europe.

6. *Sack of Rome* by Sylvestre (1890)

7. Augustine picks up on the Bible's BOOK OF REVELATION, which speaks of the *"Heavenly Jerusalem"* or the New Jerusalem, a better place than this earth.

This New Jerusalem becomes an important theme for the seventeenth century New England Puritans inspired to create it in America. John Winthrop, first governor of the Massachusetts Bay Colony, gave his famous "City on a Hill" sermon in 1630, extolling the ideal.

John of Patmos watches the descent of the New Jerusalem from God in a fourteenth century tapestry

Founding New Jerusalem

John Winthrop

MIXING THE CITY OF GOD AND THE CITY OF MAN: WHEN THE CHURCH *WAS* THE STATE

After Rome's fall, there was little struggle between church and state because there was no state. For the most part, kings—such as they were—ruled with personal oaths of allegiance.[1]

As for anything resembling government, the church was *it*. For one thing, clerics were the only ones who could read and write, and bureaucracy cannot run without writing.[2]

This is not to say that power struggles did not exist between kings and the church, only that this was not the institutionalized struggle that we mean today when we speak of the separation of church and state.

A famous event in medieval history illustrates the complicated relationship between the church and rulers: Pope Leo III's crowning Charlemagne as emperor.[3]

On Christmas day 800, Pope Leo III "surprised"

---

1. With feudal kings, government was personal and based on the oath of fealty (from Latin "*fidelitas*," or "faithfulness")—a pledge of allegiance of one person to another. The oath was typically made upon a religious object such as a Bible or a saint's relic, thus binding the oath-taker before God. *See* **Chapter 5 of** *Bills, Quills, and Stills*, **(Constitution Press re-release 2017).** In medieval Europe, fealty was sworn between two people: the obliged person ("vassal") and a person of rank ("lord").

2. Judges and university professors, all of whom used to be clerics, still wear clerical "priest" robes, as do graduating university students. We get our modern word "clerk" from "cleric." *Cleric*, THE CATHOLIC ENCYCLOPEDIA, http://www.newadvent.org/cathen/04049b.htm (last visited May 13, 2007).

Justice Oliver Wendell Holmes, Jr. in his robes.

3. Overlapping Politics. Ostensibly, this is a painting of Leo III crowning Charlemagne Holy Roman emperor in 800. But the painting has more to do with sixteenth century politics, because the pope is really Leo X, with Francis I depicted as Charlemagne.

The Coronation of Charlemagne by Raphael (c. 1517)

Roland pledges to Charlemagne

Charlemagne with the imperial crown, making him not just king of the Franks but *imperator augustus*, the first Holy Roman emperor.[4] This was an event loaded with symbolism and politics. Pope Leo was asserting that the pope could assume the power to recognize—i.e., select—the emperor, a very different deal from the one Emperor Constantine worked out four centuries earlier.[5]

But despite Leo's claims, the church still lived in a violent world.[6] In exchange for the church's recognition and legitimacy, kings and lords protected the church.

Only later did the Church gain more overt political power. In 1057, Pope Gregory VII declared that the pope was supreme not only over other bishops but also over secular authorities:

> *"Emperors must kiss the feet of the bishop of Rome."*[7]

Most emperors, kings, and other potentates did not comply. But what gave the church its real power was what it had to offer.[8]

---

4. Voltaire once quipped, *"[t]he Holy Roman Empire was neither Holy, nor Roman, nor an Empire."*

6. Charlemagne in 772 aids Pope Hadrian I (Leo's predecessor) with military assistance.

5. Compare Charlemagne getting the crown from Pope Leo with Constantine being crowned by the city of Constantinople.

Who got to put the crown on was still an issue a thousand years later when Napoleon crowned himself and then Josefina with the Pope and the church passively looking on.

Napoleon Crowning Josefina by David (1805–08)

7. *Quoted in* Harold J. Berman, *Religious Foundations of Law in the West: An Historical Perspective*, 1 J.L. & Religion 3, 6 (1983). Before Gregory VII, the emperor was the head of the church and "vicar of Christ," with the pope being just the "vicar of Saint Peter." For most of history before this, the emperor actually chose the pope, not the other way around.

Pope Gregory VII

8. Secular power began to support church decrees as when the Emperor Honorius provided in 412 that no clergyman should be accused criminally except before a bishop. Charlemagne later affirmed that a litigant could transfer his cause from a secular court to an ecclesiastical tribunal. Charles P. Sherman, *A Brief History of Imperial Roman Canon Law*, 7 Cal. L. Rev. 93, 102–04 (1918).

The church was the center of learning, culture, and law.[1] It invented universities, first to study theology but then other disciplines.[2] The church nurtured great scholars, jurists, philosophers, and theologians, who took old legal texts and systems and synthesized them.[3]

The church offered *law* to the people of western Europe.[4] Kings rose or fell, and empires grew or shrank, but the church unified the whole and endured. What this meant in practical terms is that nearly everyone in Europe lived under at least two legal systems:

the emperor's (or king's, or baron's, or lord's, etc.) and the church's. As this system of law evolved, each checked the other so that no power was absolute.

As we will see, Henry VIII of England eliminated the whole system. The later

1. Berman, *Religious Foundations*, at 3 ("*For over eight hundred years, from the late eleventh to the early twentieth century, law in the West was supported by, and in many respects based on, religious beliefs, both Roman Catholic and Protestant.*").

4. The first German law book, THE SACHSEN-SPIEGEL (1220), says that "*God is himself law; and therefore law is dear to him.*" *Quoted in* Berman, *Religious Foundations*, at 12.

5. Berman, *Religious Foundations*, at 10. This church-state legal system with concurrent, concordant, and competing jurisdiction is a precursor to American federalism and the separation of powers. *See* **Chapter 9: The Ninth Amendment: Still a Mystery after All These Years; Chapter 10: "Are You Talkin' to Me?": Just Who Are Those "People" in the Tenth Amendment?**

2. Around 1087, the church created the first university at Bologna. Berman, *Religious Foundations*, at 7.

Medieval meeting of doctors at the University of Paris

3. The greatest was Peter Abelard (1079–1142), who first used the term "theology" in the modern sense of a systematic study of God and coined the term "positive law" to refer to enacted law rather than custom or natural law. Berman, *Religious Foundations*, at 8, n.7; *see also* WILL DURANT, THE AGE OF FAITH: A HISTORY OF MEDIEVAL CIVILIZATION—CHRISTIAN, ISLAMIC, AND JUDAIC—FROM CONSTANTINE TO DANTE: A.D. 325–1300, at 931–48 (1950). He was also famous for his love of Heloise. Artists have painted them for centuries, and their affair was made into the film STEALING HEAVEN (1988). Lovers still visit their tomb in the Paris cemetery.

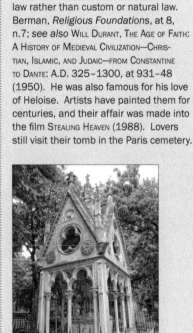

Abelard and Heloise's tomb

Abelard and Heloïse depicted in a fourteenth century manuscript

Abaelardus and Heloïse Surprised by Fulbert by Vanguard (1819)

Abelard and His Pupil, Héloïse by Blair (1882)

constitutional "revolution-aries," like our Founding Fathers, put it back.[5]

SPEAKING OF THE CHURCH IN ENGLAND

One day in sixth century Rome, Pope Gregory the

Great saw tall, blond, and fair-skinned slaves for sale. With pity and curiosity he asked after them.

"They are Angles," replied someone.

"Not Angles but angels," reflected Gregory.

In 595, Gregory commissioned a Benedictine monk, later known as Saint Augustine of Canterbury, to convert the pagan King Æthelberht of Kent.[6] Thus was born the English Catholic Church.

6. Christianity actually came to Britain well before 300 AD. In Roman times, this Celtic Christianity had its own distinctive culture and Greek scholarship. See THOMAS CAHILL, HOW THE IRISH SAVED CIVILIZATION: THE UNTOLD STORY OF IRELAND'S HEROIC ROLE FROM THE FALL OF ROME TO THE RISE OF MEDIEVAL EUROPE (1995), for an account of Celtic/Irish Christianity and its relationship with the newer Roman/Augustine Christianity. In the fifth century, non-Christian Germanic tribes invaded Britain. The Angles, Saxons, and Jutes conquered the native Celtic Christians and drove them into Cornwall, Wales, Scotland, Ireland, and Brittany, a peninsula in France.

The King Arthur stories have their origin in a Celtic leader who resisted the invaders and ended up being a Hollywood favorite. See e.g., EXCALIBUR (Orion Pictures 1981) KING ARTHUR (Touchstone Pictures 1994) KNIGHTS OF THE ROUND TABLE (MGM 1953).

Richard Burton and Roddy McDowall in the Arthurian Play CAMELOT.

Saint Gregory and Saint Augustine

British stamps commemorating Saint Augustine baptizing King Ethelbert and establishing Canterbury Cathedral, Saint Augustine's Abbey, and Saint Martin's Church

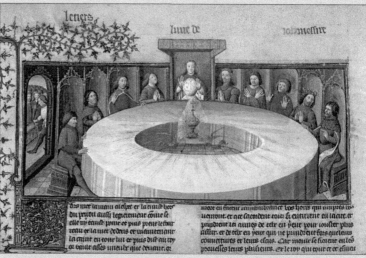
A fifteenth century depiction of Arthur, the Round Table, and the Holy Grail

Centuries later, Rome cut a deal with William the Bastard for his invasion of England. William promised that if he won the English crown, the church could have greater power.[1]

In 1066, William won and became William *the Conqueror*—far better then being William *the Bastard* for all of history.[2]

Before the Norman Conquest, England had no separate ecclesiastical courts or independent ecclesiastical law.[3] The Norman king's introduction of church courts planted the seeds of the power struggle that was to play out over centuries, namely:

- Does king or pope or archbishop name a prelate or priest?

- Where are people tried, in the king's courts or the ecclesiastical courts?

- What about clergy who violate civil law? [4]

Over history, jurisdiction between the king's courts and the church courts was very fluid. For example, stealing and brawling were common-law crimes, but if they were done in a church, they became ecclesiastical crimes. On these and other questions, sometimes the king won and sometimes the church won.

But despite the church's jurisdictional power over court cases, the crown still usually controlled the church leadership. The archbishop of Canterbury,

William the Bastard

1. David Howarth, 1066: The Year of the Conquest 100–03 (1977) (discussing William's deal with the church and the trumped-up legal argument in Rome against his rival, Harold). As Howarth summed up, "*of all the novel weapons the Conqueror brought, the most effective was not the archery or the horsemen but the papal banner.*" Howarth at 197.

Odo rallies the troops with his club

An arrow in the eye kills Harold

2. William's half brother was Bishop Odo of Bayeux (c. 1036–97). He was either fourteen or nineteen years old when William made him bishop of Bayeux. Hardly a man of peace, he participated at Hastings and probably commissioned the Bayeux tapestry, showing himself fully engaged in the battle. But because he was a churchman he could not "*shed blood*" and thus used a mace or club rather than a sword. See Danny Danziger & John Gillingham, 1215: The Year of Magna Carta 102–03 (2003); Colin Rhys Lovell, English Constitutional and Legal History 55 (1962). Odo led the church in England after the Normans took over.

3. Levy, Origins of the Fifth Amendment 43 (1968). Under the Anglo-Saxons, bishops sat as judges. Regarding the Normans establishing separate church courts, see Lovell at 69.

4. Benefit of Clergy. This allowed churchmen to claim they were outside the king's jurisdiction and receive trial under canon law by compurgation, with the likely punishment being penance rather than hanging. It eventually passed into the common law and became a factor in the Boston Massacre trials. See **Chapter 8 of Bills, Quills, and Stills, (Constitution Press re-release 2017).**

Tonsured monk

Boston Massacre

for example, was primate of England but was also a vassal of the king and thus remained the king's tenant.[5]

This was the backdrop to the struggle between King Henry II and his former friend, the archbishop of Canterbury, Thomas Becket.

"WON'T SOMEBODY RID ME OF THIS DAMNED PRIEST!"

Thus cried King Henry II about Thomas Becket. Henry's knights took him at his word and splattered the archbishop's brains at vespers on December 20, 1170.[6]

Becket had been Henry's great friend and chancellor. Henry made him archbishop of Canterbury on June 3, 1162. (To avoid the fact that Becket was not yet a priest, he was ordained the day before!) But their relationship soured as Becket began to take his job seriously, asserting the church's independence, jurisdiction, and tax exemptions.[7]

Henry was always trying to expand his power, organization, and control. Before 1166, for instance, both a bishop and the king's magistrate presided over most English courts. In that year (one hundred years after the Battle of Hastings), Henry passed new legislation at the Assize of Clarendon placing the king's courts exclusively under royal authority.

Becket's defiance of Henry led to his murder in 1170. Henry got the blame, probably deservedly so. He did public penance, including a scourging at the archbishop's tomb.[8] Although

5. Lovell at 67. High churchmen swore to the king for their "temporalities" before they had their spiritual investiture. *Id.* at 75. During this period, income from church lands in England was conservatively around £80,000 per year. Danziger & Gillingham at 131. What this really means in today's dollars is anyone's guess—but we know it was a lot!

6. Earliest known portrayal of Becket's murder. The murderers were William de Tracy, Reginald FitzUrse, Hugh de Morville, and Richard le Bret. See Danziger & Gillingham at 127–29 for a brief account of the Becket story and church/state power struggle. Becket sealed his fate when he called FitzUrse a "pimp." *Id.* at128; *see also* Lovell at 94–99.

7. Henry and Becket disputing.

8. The story is still high drama. See T. S. Eliot's play Murder in the Cathedral (1935) as well as the movie Becket (Paramount Pictures 1964), with Richard Burton as Becket and Peter O'Toole as Henry II. As for Henry's life and loves in film, see The Lion in Winter (Universal Pictures 1968), in which O'Toole again plays Henry, sparring with Katherine Hepburn's Eleanor of Aquitaine. Although these works have several historical inaccuracies, they make for good drama.

Page from The Canterbury Tales

Becket's shrine at Canterbury became the main pilgrimage site in England, with Geoffrey Chaucer's The Canterbury Tales, set in the fourteenth century, two hundred years after Becket's murder, centering on the stories of pilgrims:

"When the sweet showers of April have pierced to the root the dryness of March and bathed every vein in moisture by which strength are the flowers brought forth then people long to go on pilgrimages to renowned shrines in various distant lands, and palmers to seek foreign shores. And especially from every shire's end in England they make their way to Canterbury, to seek the holy blessed martyr who helped them when they were sick."

In A Knight's Tale (Columbia Pictures 2001), Paul Bettany plays "Geoffrey Chaucer," who will later write "The Knight's Tale" as one of The Canterbury Tales.

the church purged Henry of guilt for Becket's murder, he had to allow the church's privileges to continue. Becket was later canonized.[1]

After Henry II, the church continued as an *imperium in imperio* (a kingdom within a kingdom), with independent courts appealing to Rome.[2] Church courts also had different procedures, such as oral, sworn testimony, proof by paper (i.e., sworn depositions), and specialized pleading.

Henry II did not like the new deal. For example, in 1173, he ostensibly honored the ideal of free election for prelates when he wrote the following to the monks of Saint Swithin's Priory at Winchester:

> *"I order you to hold a free election . . . nevertheless I forbid you to elect anyone save Richard my clerk."*[3]

This power struggle between church and state would continue through the centuries.[4]

MAGNA CARTA AND FREEDOM OF RELIGION

Under Henry's son, King John,[5] the church-state power struggle played out in grand fashion.

In 1205, archbishop of Canterbury Hubert died, and everyone claimed the right to fill his job.[6]

King John's insistence that he could fill the job led Pope Innocent III in Rome to put England under "interdiction," which meant that the clergy went on strike.[7]

For six years, from 1208 to 1214, no masses were said and no church bells rang. John did not care, because he kept all the revenue from

---

1. Three centuries later, a similar drama played out between Saint Thomas More, named after Saint Thomas Becket, and also the chancellor to a king Henry, this time Henry VIII. On More's echo of Becket, see Lovell at 263.

Three years after More's death, Henry VIII summoned the bones of Thomas Becket to appear before him. Sadakat Kadri, The Trial: A History, from Socrates to O.J. Simpson 168 (2005). When Becket's bones failed to appear, Henry had them hanged on a gibbet, burned to ashes, and shot from a cannon. Henry also stole all the contributed valuables from Becket's shrine, including just under 5,000 ounces of gold, 5,286 ounces of silver, 4,452 ounces of gilt plate, 840 ounces of parcel gilt, and a precious stone with gold angels that Henry made into a thumb ring. Kurt von S. Kynell, Saxon and Medieval Antecedents of the English Common Law 179–80, 185 n.35 (2000).

Pope Paul III later excommunicated Henry, partly because he "*surpass[ed] the ferocity of any heathen people, who, even when they have conquered their enemies in war, are not accustomed to outrage their bodies.*" Kadri at 168.

2. Lovell at 95–96.

3. Danziger & Gillingham at 131.

4. A "prelate" is a high-ranking member of the clergy, usually a bishop or abbot. The word comes from Latin "*prælatus*," the past participle of "*præferre*," literally, "carry before," or "to be set above, or over," or "to prefer."

Prelates in the Catholic and other churches often wear mitres during ceremonies, which the chess piece, the bishop, symbolizes.

5. King John is the great wimp of English history. See **Chapter 6 of Bills, Quills, and Stills,** (Constitution Press re-release 2017).

King John

vacant bishoprics (most of which he never returned). He also stopped paying the clergy their salaries under the theory that because they were not doing their job, they should not get paid.[8]

All this showed the king's power to control the church. Under feudalism, a priest was roughly equivalent to a knight and had a little fief called a parish. Ultimately, his holding of his parish depended not on his flock but on the next higher person in the feudal chain. The king was at the top, which meant that there was no real separation of church and state.

The pope was unable to get John to change until he was about to authorize King Phillip of France to invade England with the church's blessing. John submitted and accepted the pope's guy, Stephen Langton, as archbishop of Canterbury. The pope told Phillip to hold off, which he did, for a while.

Eventually, John's barons, the church, and the king of France all aligned against John. In 1215, the barons got him to sign and swear to *Magna Carta*, the first document in our constitutional history.[9] Stephen Langton wrote and negotiated most of it, which may account for the first clause:

"The English church shall be free, and shall have its rights undiminished and its liberties unimpaired."[10]

From then on, English kings swore to *Magna Carta* as part of the coronation oath, as Henry VIII did three hundred years later in 1509. Henry later ignored his oath by making himself the pope of England.

But first an obscure monk named Martin Luther changed the world forever.

6. In a nutshell here is what happened:
- Archbishop Hubert died;
- The Canterbury monks and bishops wanted to vote for his replacement;
- King John got them all to wait (and incidentally got to keep all the revenues from Canterbury's lands in the meantime);
- Some of the monks went ahead and secretly elected a guy named Reginald, who went to Rome;
- The rest of the monks thought that was not a good idea, especially after the king showed up, and they elected another guy named John;
- Back in Rome, Pope Innocent III rejected the monks' claim to have had a vote and invalidated both elections;
- Pope Innocent put in his own guy named Stephen Langton;
- John rejected this and would not let Stephen take the job;
- Innocent put all of England under interdiction, closing all the churches for six years, from 1208 to 1214.
DANZIGER & GILLINGHAM at 132.

Archbishop Hubert Walter's tomb at Canterbury

7. Pope Innocent III.

8. DANZIGER & GILLINGHAM at 136–37. John also kidnapped all the "wives" and mistresses of the priests and would not release them until the priests paid him so that they could continue sinning.

9. DANZIGER & GILLINGHAM at 139. We will hear a lot more about *Magna Carta* in other chapters.

10. *Quoted in* DANZIGER & GILLINGHAM at 125. Langton probably was the one who preserved *Magna Carta* in the church archives.

Magna Carta

LUTHER AND CALVIN SAYING WHAT THEY BELIEVED

On October 31, 1517, Martin Luther nailed on the church door at Wittenberg, Germany, the Ninety-Five Theses, or questions on Catholic theology and practice.[1]

For centuries, the Roman Church had taught that with reason and free will, a man could live a good life, and by combining faith and good deeds achieve salvation.[2] The good deeds could be making a pilgrimage or giving alms to the poor or other charity.[3] By Luther's day, though, this teaching had become corrupted into the great moneymaker of selling indulgences.[4]

Luther strongly disputed Rome's claim that one could buy freedom from God's punishment. He taught instead that salvation did not come from good works but only from God's grace.

Regarding the relationship of church and state, Luther picked up on Saint Augustine's "city of God" and "city of man" theme. After all, Luther started as an Augustinian monk.[5]

In Luther's thinking, there were two kingdoms. A person could *not* work his way from the "earthly kingdom" into the "heavenly kingdom" because only God's grace could allow it. Still, though, a Christian in the earthly kingdom must

---

1. Martin Luther and a printed copy of the Ninety-Five Theses.

2. Berman, *Religious Foundations*, at 15.

3. Pilgrimage as a journey to redress sin played out in Kingdom of Heaven (20th Century Fox 2005).

Saint Peter's Basilica, the architectural and artistic marvel that prompted the Protestant Reformation

4. Indulgences were a great product for the church to sell because it could always make more! What you could buy was time out of purgatory for a relative or even yourself. Because only God knew how much time you had in purgatory, you could never know if you bought enough time out! So, the church could keep selling you ten years or one thousand years, depending on how badly you thought you had behaved.

A Dominican preacher, Johann Tetzel (1465–1519), had a great sales pitch: "*As soon as a coin in the coffer rings/ the soul from purgatory springs.*" His sales in Germany to raise money to build Saint Peter's Basilica in Rome prompted Luther to protest. Luther's Thesis 86 asked, "*Why does the pope, whose wealth today is greater than the wealth of the richest Crassus, build the basilica of Saint Peter with the money of poor believers rather than with his own money?*" Regarding Martin Luther see Luther (MGM 2003) a biopic starring Joseph Fiennes as Luther and Alfred Molina as Tetzel

5. The Augustinians still exist as religious orders of men and women in the Catholic Church following the Rule of Saint Augustine. Erasmus, Luther's contemporary, was also an Augustinian. As we will see, Erasmus was a great friend of Thomas More and a powerful voice for humanistic reform *within* the Catholic Church.

Leaving aside who was right about God, you cannot help but wonder how much bloodshed the world would have avoided had people both in and out of the Catholic Church chosen Erasmus's path of reform rather than Luther's.

Other Augustinians included a couple of popes and mystics as well as Gregor Mendel, whose 1850 to 1860 studies of pea pod plants in the monastery garden made him the "father of genetics."

Mendel

work to follow God. Thus, politics and law were not paths to grace and faith (as Rome taught), but grace and faith were paths to right politics and law.[6]

John Calvin (1509–64) jumped into the Protestant Reformation around 1530 and, like Luther, taught the doctrine of two kingdoms. But his concept of church and state expanded from Luther's community of the faithful to actual control of the state.

Calvin's "fellowship of active believers" was the seat of truth, qualified to control not only worship but also society's morals.[7] The Calvinist view of law was that it was to "*teach*" the faithful, as well as everyone else, the right path.[8]

The Calvinists expanded on these ideas of government and created theocracies in places like Geneva, Switzerland. As we will see, the English Calvinists, also known

as the Puritans, sparked the English Civil Wars in the 1640s.[9] These same Pilgrim Puritans came to America to set up their New Jerusalem.

Luther respected civil authority and accepted a world where the prince was a *de facto* head of the church.[10] The Calvinists, however, sought to *establish* both church and state as a check on each other.

Luther as a young Augustinian monk

Erasmus of Rotterdam

6. Berman, *Religious Foundations*, at 15–17.

John Calvin

7. Berman, *Religious Foundations*, at 26, noting that the Calvinistic concept of law differed from the Catholic notion of law as something *given*. For the Calvinist, law was something *useful*.

9. Berman, *Religious Foundations*, at 27.

10. Berman, *Religious Foundations*, at 18.

8. Berman, *Religious Foundations*, at 30 ("*It was, of course, in Puritan New England more than anywhere else that the concept of reformation of the world was combined with the doctrine of the 'didactic' or 'pedagogical' use of the law to impose heavy criminal sanctions—indeed the death penalty—for moral offenses, especially those of a sexual or religious nature.*"). THE SCARLET LETTER was about pedagogy. NATHANIEL HAWTHORNE, THE SCARLET LETTER (1850). Set in seventeenth century Puritanical Boston, the novel tells of Hester Prynne, who gives birth after adultery, refuses to name the father, and struggles to create a new life of repentance and dignity. Several movie adaptations exist, including THE SCARLET LETTER (Hollywood Pictures 1995).

Classic Comics version of THE SCARLET LETTER

PRESSING RELIGION: LUTHER PUBLISHED, AND PUBLISHED, AND THUS DID NOT PERISH

To know God and grace, a man should read his Bible, said Luther, who obviously could no longer rely on the Pope or the Roman Church. So Luther translated the Bible into German, the language of his people. It exploded on the scene.

There are many causes of the Protestant Reformation, but in ages past, the Catholic Church had confronted pagans, heretics, schisms, religious movements, and constant challenges to its authority.[1]

---

1. For example, there were the Paulicans from the fifth through seventh centuries, the Bogomils in the eighth century, and the Cathars of eleventh through thirteenth centuries, who form the backdrop to Dan Brown's THE DAVINCI CODE (2003) and the subsequent film, THE DAVINCI CODE (Columbia Pictures 2006).

Later came the Joachimites of the thirteenth century, and the Apostolic Brethern and Dulcinian heresies that form the backdrop of Umberto Eco's THE NAME OF THE ROSE (1980) and the film, THE NAME OF THE ROSE (20th Century Fox 1986).

Eco's book is a good primer on medieval philosophy and theology.

2. And with printing, the books themselves became ever more dangerous.

Book burning did not start with the printing press. In fact, before printing book burning was more effective because books had to be hand copied, so replacing books was a long, laborious task.

Disputation between Saint Dominic and Cathers by Berruguete (fifteenth century), shows the story of Cathar and Saint Dominic's books thrown on a fire but Dominic's did not burn, showing the truth of his teachings. This story shows the early Dominican desire to convert heretics by persuasion.

Disputation between Saint Dominic and Cathers by Berruguete

In 1644, John Milton wrote against the destruction of books and their ideas:
™*He who kills a man kills a reasonable creature, God's image; but he who destroys a good book, kills reason itself, kills the image of God, as it were, in the eye.*" Books, moreover, "*are not absolutely dead things, but do contain a potency of life in them to be as active as that soul was whose progeny they are.*" Thus for Milton, destroying a book is a "*kind of homicide,*" "*sometimes a martyrdom,*" even "*a kind of massacre.*" Witte, *Milton*, at

John Milton

1592–93, *quoting* AREOPAGITICA: A SPEECH OF MR. JOHN MILTON FOR THE LIBERTY OF UNLICENSED PRINTING TO THE PARLIAMENT OF ENGLAND (1644). But though Milton defends books and their ideas perhaps better than anyone else, his defense also shows why book burning did not end. People who are willing to kill for their ideology will just as easily kill a book: ™*On the evening of May 10, 1933, some four and a half months after Hitler became Chancellor, there occurred in Berlin a scene which had not been witnessed in the Western world since the late Middle Ages. At about midnight a torchlight parade of thousands of students ended at a square . . . opposite the University of Berlin. Torches were put to a huge pile of books that had been gathered there, and as the flames enveloped them more books were thrown on the fire until some twenty thousand had been consumed. Similar scenes took place in several other cities. The book burning had begun.*"
. . . Dr. Joseph Goebbels, the new propaganda minister, who from now on was to put German culture into a Nazi strait jacket, addressed the students as the burning books turned to ashes. The soul of the German people can again express itself. These flames not only illuminate the final end of an old era; they also light up the new. Id.
WILLIAM L. SHIRER, THE RISE AND FALL OF THE THIRD REICH: A HISTORY OF NAZI GERMANY 333 (1950, 1960). One of the books the Nazi's

burned was the play ALMANSOR: A TRAGEDY (1823) by Heinrich Heine, who referred to the Spanish Inquisition's burning of the Muslim Qur'an and wrote "*[w]here they burn books, so too will they in the end burn human beings.*" The Nazis proved him right with the Holocaust. For reference to Heine's quote, see United States Holocaust Memorial Museum, http://www.ushmm.org/research/library/faq/details.php?topic=06#quote_heine (last visited Aug. 21, 2010).

Ray Bradbury's FAHRENHEIT 451 (1951) is

Heinrich Heine

a cautionary tale of a world where books are burned to control ideas and people. According to Bradbury, "451" is the temperature at which book paper burns. (This is actually not accurate, with the actual temperature being closer to 450 degrees Celsius, which would be 842 degrees Fahrenheit, but Bradbury thought "Fahrenheit" made a better title.) Bradbury wrote it during the Cold War to critique American society. *See also* FAHRENHEIT 451 (Universal Pictures 1966).

There is a book burning in the movie PLEASANTVILLE (New Line Cinema 1998), which makes the point that new and different ideas are not always "pleasant," but they are necessary for any world with color and beauty that is worth living in. As for book burning in America, the New York Society for the Suppression of Vice, founded in 1873 by the antipornography crusader Anthony Comstock, advocated book burning and even inscribed it on its seal. Comstock burned tons of books that he considered "lewed" and successfully lobbied the U.S. Congress to pass the Comstock Act, 17 Stat. 598, on March 3, 1873, making it illegal to send any "obscene, lewd, and/or lascivious" materials through the mail, includ-

So what made Luther, and later Calvin, different?

It was the printing press.[2]

A mere generation before Luther, Johann Gutenberg started printing.[3] And Gutenberg's first book in 1455 was the Bible.[4]

In a very real sense, the Protestant Reformation was about printing: bibles, tracts, teachings, charters, covenants, institutes, and books. They were best sellers and gave men like Luther a living after they left the monastery.[5]

The press made religion, and religion made the press, underscoring why the First Amendment is about both.

---

ing contraceptive devices and information.

We can hope that the Internet may have

made book burnings a thing of the past; you cannot burn the whole World Wide Web. But countries like China that limit access to the web are trying to do the same thing. According to Amnesty International, China blocks all information regarding subjects such as the Tiananmen Square protests and has the largest recorded number of imprisoned journalists and cyberdissidents in the world. *China: No Investigation, No Redress and Still No Freedom of Speech! Human Rights Activists Targeted for Discussing the Tiananmen Crackdown*, AMNESTY INTERNATIONAL, http://www.amnesty.org/en/library/info/ASA17/025/2010/en (last visited Aug. 15, 2010).

3. Gutenberg did not invent printing or the printing press, which existed long before using carved wooden blocks. What he invented was a practical way of making movable type with a metal alloy and a hand mould. Movable type allows the printer to place precast letters on a block that he can then "press" on paper. This is done for as many copies as needed, and then the printer

Johann Gutenberg

reorders the type to press the next page. (This, of course, is the origin of "the Press" as the First Amendment uses the term.) In a day a printer can print thousands of identical copies of a page that would have taken medieval monks weeks to inscribe.

A case of cast metal type pieces and typeset matter in a composing stick

The 1959 Xerox 914, the first plain paper photocopier using xerography (from Greek "xeros" ("dry") and "graphos" ("writing").

Cast metal type

A woodblock from 1568 showing one printer removing a page while another inks the text blocks

4 Gutenberg's Bible was a prop in the apocalyptic THE DAY AFTER TOMORROW (20th Century Fox 2004), clutched by the librarian, Jeremy: who wants to save one little piece of "Western Civilization".

Gutenberg first page

5. The Typewriter. Think of the typewriter as a little printing press invented in the 1870s. A typewriter is a machine with movable type. Instead of putting lead type on a big block it has little levers called keys that you press in the order you want. Also, instead of having to ink all the type on the block beforehand, the typewriter's keys hit an ink tape just before hitting the paper, transferring the ink from the tape onto the page. Thus, the type never touches the paper, only the ink tape, which advances each time you push a key. The standard layout of the typewriter keyboard—QWERTY—has a near alphabetical sequence on the "home row."

But, by design, QWERTY is not the most efficient layout possible because it requires the typist to move his or her fingers between rows for the most common letters. This slows the typist to prevent the key bars from jamming. Now that word processors and computers have replaced the typewriter, there is no need for the QWERTY layout other than that we all learned it.

HENRY VIII: WHEN DESIRE BECAME DOGMA

Finally back to Henry! [1]

One thing to remember about Henry VIII is that at heart he was a conservative Catholic all his life. He just decided to be Pope of England. In matters of heresy, both before and after he broke with Rome, Henry differed from other leaders of his time only by the greater severity of his intolerance. [2]

Before Henry's "great matter"—that is, his divorce from Catharine of Aragon—Pope Leo X had recognized him for writing, with Sir Thomas More's help, ASSERTIO SEPTEM SACRAMENTORUM MARTINUM LUTHERUM (DECLARATION OF THE

1. *Henry VIII* by Hans Holbein (1540)
This Holbein painting shows a man bursting with charm and good nature. Trusting in that could cost you your head. Thomas More's biographer and son-in-law, William Roper, recounted a telling conversation with More:
"Roper: *How happy he was whom the King had so familiarly entertained . . .*
More: *I thank our Lord, son, I find his Grace my very good Lord indeed . . . Howbeit, son Roper, I may tell thee I have no cause to be proud thereof **for if my head could win him a castle in France . . . it should not fail to fall.**"*
ROPER at 13 (emphasis added). Roper wrote twenty years after More's execution in 1535. But adding credence to this conversation is what happened

William Roper

Holbein's sketch of More

two days after Henry's coronation in 1510. Henry VIII had arrested his father, Henry VII's two most unpopular but loyal ministers, Sir Richard Empson and Edmund Dudley. Henry VIII had them groundlessly charged with high treason and executed. They, like More, were lawyers.

2. Henry reserved for himself in the Act of Supremacy the power to "*repress and extirp all errors, heresies, and other enormities.*" LEVY, FIFTH AMENDMENT, at 68–69.

Sir Richard Empson (left) Henry VII, and Sir Edmund Dudley

Dickens at his desk in 1858

Charles Dickens wrote A CHILD'S HISTORY OF ENGLAND for his own children and it became part of the English school curriculum. Summing up Henry VIII, Dickens wrote, "*The plain truth is, that he was a most intolerable ruffian, a disgrace to human nature, and a blot of blood and grease upon the History of England.*" III CHARLES DICKENS, A CHILD'S HISTORY OF ENGLAND 59 (1853), *available at* http://www.archive. org/stream/childshistoryofe03di ckrich#page/58/mode/2up (last visited Nov. 7, 2009).

3. And Henry VIII is still a star. Shakespeare started it with his play, THE FAMOUS HISTORY OF THE LIFE OF KING HENRY VIII (1613). In 1613 a cannon shot fired for special effect during a performance of HENRY VIII burned the original Globe Theatre to the ground. There is also an opera HENRY VIII (1883), by Camille Saint-Saëns. Henry is a character in Mark Twain's THE PRINCE AND THE PAUPER (1881). Charles Laughton won an Oscar for THE PRIVATE LIFE OF HENRY VIII (United Artists 1933), and Robert Shaw was bombastic in A MAN FOR ALL SEASONS (Columbia Pictures 1966), which won Best Picture in 1966. Television works have included *Henry VIII*, a two-part serial (Granada Television 2003) and the dumbed-down, sexed-up *The Tudors* (Showtime 2007–present).

Charles Laughton and Binnie Barnes in THE PRIVATE LIFE OF HENRY VIII (United Artists 1983)

4. You can still see the "FD" for *fidei defensor* on British coins today. Why Henry and his successors kept the title is odd. If they did not recognize the Pope as anything more than the "Bishop of Rome," why keep the title that he bequeathed?

Leo X

Never underestimate Henry's capacity for self-justification.
As for Leo X and his cousin Clement VII, see E.R. CHAMBERLIN, THE BAD POPES (1969), a slim history that nevertheless devotes a chapter to each.

SEVEN SACRAMENTS AGAINST MARTIN LUTHER). This book was a best seller and made Henry the first king to ever publish a book—again, the mix of press and religion![3]

Because of this book, Pope Leo dubbed him "defender of the faith" (*fidei defensor*), which to this day is still one of a British monarch's titles.[4]

But two popes later, Clement VII (who was Leo X's cousin) did not grant Henry the divorce he sought to rid himself of Queen Catherine of Aragon in favor of Anne Boleyn.[5]

Henry tired of appealing to Rome,[6] of Rome controlling a huge chunk of England, and of the church being a separate government. And, of course, he tired of having to wait to marry Anne Boleyn.[7]

---

5. Little of this had to do with the sanctity of marriage. At the time, Clement was a virtual prisoner of Emperor Charles V, who just happened to be Catherine of Aragon's nephew. Not wanting to see Aunt Catherine dethroned as Queen of England, Charles blocked Henry's annulment. This fiasco cost Henry's lord chancellor, Cardinal Wolsey, his job. (What good is a cardinal in your employ if you cannot get an annulment when you need one?) Anne Boleyn took a personal interest in Wolsey's demise and got his palace. En route to face the treason indictment, he died declaring "*[i]f I had served God as diligently as I have done the King, he would not have given me over in my gray hairs.*" Thomas Wolsey, THE CATHOLIC ENCYCLOPEDIA, http://www.newadvent.org/cathen/15685a.htm218 (last visited Feb. 10, 2006).

Clement VII   Charles V   Wolsey   Cranmer

6. Wolsey Couldn't Cut It! Wolsey was Lord Chancellor of England, the highest official under the king *and* papal legate (i.e., delegate), exercising the Pope's powers in England. It should have been easy for him to get Henry's annulment. Regarding Wolsey's powers of both church and state, see LOVELL at 254. He ended up sending Rome eighty petitions, all bound in the customary red tape. In the end, he could not cut through the red tape, which is the first recorded use of the expression "red tape" for bureaucratic obstacles.

Elizabeth of York holding a white (York) rose

7. To be fair, more than just lust drove Henry. He believed he needed a male heir (although the successful forty-five-year reign of his daughter Elizabeth proved him wrong). His father, Henry Tudor, came to the throne as Henry VII after defeating Richard III at Bosworth Field. Henry Tudor had a weak claim to the throne but married Edward IV's daughter, Elizabeth of York (who is the model for the Queen of Hearts in a card deck). Thus, Henry VII was able to unite the two great factions of the Lancasters, represented by the red rose, and the Yorks, represented by the white rose, thus ending the Wars of the Roses (1455–85) and giving us the red and white Tudor rose. *See generally* JOHN GILLINGHAM, THE WARS OF THE ROSES (1981). The fear of repeating the destructiveness of the Wars of the Roses drove Henry VIII and assured the complacency of a great part of England's political and religious power structure when Henry made himself Pope of England. *See* LOVELL at 255.

Henry VII holding a red (Lancaster) rose

Richard III

Wolsey trying to cut the "red tape"

York   Lancaster   Tudor

It always gnawed at European kings that the church was outside their jurisdiction and taxing power. Henry put an end to it by taking the church's entire legal jurisdiction into his own hands. Henry, who had received a superior theological education, must have thought, why not control the church?[1]

So Henry decided to be the Pope in England.[2]

To become Pope, Henry had Parliament pass the Statute in Restraint of Appeals, which ended all appeals to the Pope and made Henry the final legal authority on all religious and jurisdictional questions.[3] As justification, Henry claimed that the

English crown was imperial, and thus, like Constantine, he wanted to establish (i.e., control) the church.

Henry later had Parliament pass the Act of Supremacy of 1534, which made him

"the only supreme head in earth of the Church of England called Anglicana

---

1. Henry was Henry VII and Elizabeth of York's second son after Arthur. They trained him for the church, probably to be Archbishop of Canterbury. Arthur died in 1502, leaving Henry to take the throne and, because Henry VII did not want to see his political alliance with Spain harmed, he made his son, Henry (later Henry VIII), take Arthur's "wife" Catherine of Aragon. Even though Arthur and Catherine never consummated the marriage, Henry VII had to arrange a dispensation from Rome to allow the marriage to Prince Henry. When Cath-

erine later did not give Henry VIII a male heir, he made himself believe, and got his paid churchmen and scholars to argue, that it was God's punishment for marrying his brother's wife against *Leviticus* 18:16: *"Thou shalt not uncover the nakedness of thy brother's wife: it is thy brother's nakedness."* And *Leviticus* 20:21: *"If a man shall take his brother's wife, it is an unclean thing . . . they shall be childless."* Thus, God clearly wanted Henry to marry his new inamorata, Anne Boleyn.

Holbein's original sketch of More

4. Act of Supremacy, 1534, 26 Hen. 8, c. 1, *available* at http:// tudorhistory. org/primary/ supremacy. html (last visited Feb. 10, 2006).

5. *See* John Witte, Jr., *Tax Exemption of Church Property: Historical Anomaly or Valid Constitutional Practice?* 64 S. CAL. L. REV. 363, 364–69 (1991) (noting that *"the Tudor monarchs had consolidated their authority over religion and the church and subjected them to comprehensive ecclesiastical laws enforceable by both common law and commissary courts"*).

2. Regarding Henry's establishment of the Church of England, *see* LOVELL at 253–70.

Arthur Tudor

Catherine

Henry

3. Otherwsie known as the Ecclesiastical Appeals Act, 1532, 24 Hen. 8, c. 12.

Henry had Parliament doing a lot, making his reign one of the milestones in the growth of parliamentary supremacy and even democracy. But Henry was no democrat! He controlled parliament.

Other Parliaments had appointed kings in the past, such as the election

of King Henry IV on October 13, 1399, dispossessing King Richard. At the start of Henry VIII's reign, however, Henry insisted he was the *anointed* king: from God to pope to me! He later found it far more useful and flexible being the *appointed* king: from God to Parliament to me! *See generally* LOVELL at 256.

The shadowy Richard Rich

This all figured in Thomas More's trial in 1535, when Richard Rich testified that More said that *"Parliament could not make the king the head of the church,"* which was malicious treason.

6. Portraits of **Catherine** when Henry married her and how she looked when he divorced her.

Catherine was eight years older than the forty-two-year-old Henry, while Anne Boleyn was in her early twenties and looked pretty good to Henry. Although she was only queen for three years, from 1533 to 1536, she gets all the press! *See, e.g.,* ANNE OF THE THOUSAND

Henry VIII and Parliament

Ecclesia, and shall have and enjoy annexed and united to the imperial crown of this realm."[4]

Before Henry, the church's bishops, abbots, and clergy had an independent income, being supported by their own lands. Although the kings would appoint many of the bishops and abbots, or somehow work out a bribe or deal with Rome to do so, after the churchmen gave the king his due, they were relatively independent. But after Henry, clergymen became the crown's employees in his "established" church.[5]

By establishing his own church, Henry was able to do a number of things:

- put away old wife Catherine of Aragon and marry his new hottie, Anne Boleyn;[6]

- gain jurisdiction and taxing power over all of England, Wales, and Ireland; and

- steal church property.[7]

Days (Universal Pictures 1969), followed by THE OTHER BOLEYN GIRL (Columbia Pictures 2008). She also figures in seasons one and two of *The Tudors* (Showtime 2007–present).

Anne Boleyn

Cromwell

Henry himself.

Ironically, Henry's profligate spending led to parliamentary democracy. By selling off the land for short-term cash, he deprived the crown of a long-term source of revenue. Henry's descendants—Edward VI, Mary, and Elizabeth—were always cash challenged, as were his Stuart successors—James I, Charles I, Charles II, and James II. The Stuarts especially had to continually call Parliaments for money just to run a government that was becoming more expensively modern. As we will see, Parliament could then "petition" for freedoms and rights.

7. Dissolution of the Monasteries: Henry's main minister, Thomas Cromwell, promised to make him *"the richest man in England."* KYNELL at 177. Henry and Cromwell did it by breaking the back of English Catholic spirituality. From 1536 to 1541, Henry made a huge amount of money by stealing monastery property.

Not only were monasteries independent of the king, they were independent of local Catholic bishops. (Accepting independence was not Henry's strong suit.) Henry disbanded 825 monasteries, nunneries, and friaries throughout England, Wales, and Ireland and took their income. He did provide a modest pension to the former members. The Act of Supremacy (1534), the First Suppression Act (1536), and the Second Suppression Act (1539) gave Henry the legal power to act.

The monasteries were indeed rich, powerful, and independent; many were not very holy.

But they were also the main providers of education and social services in England. Henry took it all for his own ends and did not replace the hospitals or alms houses. He sold their lands (on the cheap) not only to rich lords but to a whole new class of up-and-coming "Tudor gentry," who entered Parliament with a personal interest in supporting the king. Henry's annual income before he stole the church's lands was £140,000 but afterward was conservatively about £50 million in relatively modern currency (i.e., the British pound for 1910). KYNELL at 179.

Henry spent lavishly, including on the two greatest battleships of the age, the *Mary Rose* and the *Great Harry*, both of which were top heavy and unseaworthy—a good metaphor for

The *Mary Rose*

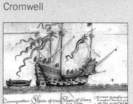

The *Great Harry* had gold cloth sails for diplomatic missions

Glastonbury Abby before Henry and now

England under Henry became a deadly place for free thought and belief.[1]

Any deviation from Henry's new religious order, most especially refusal to swear to the Act of Supremacy, threatened him.[2] No matter whether it was loyalty to the "Bishop of Rome" or belief in new Protestant doctrines, expression of dissent was too much for Henry; he sent you to the chopping block for one and to the fires of Smythfield for the other.[3] The crimes of heresy and treason became indistinguishable.[4]

Henry's friend Sir Thomas More, among many others, paid the price for Henry's acquisitiveness, passions, and quest for a male heir.

SIR THOMAS MORE: SPEAKING TRUTH TO POWER THROUGH SILENCE

Sir Thomas More was Lord Chancellor, having succeeded Cardinal Wosley, who in 1535 became one of Henry VII's earliest and most distinguished victims.[5]

---

1. Being one of Henry's wives could also be dangerous. And of Henry's wives? Just remember their fates in two trilogies: **DivorcedExecutedDied; DivorcedExecutedSurvived!**

Divorced — Catherine of Aragon; mother of the future Queen Mary.

Executed — Anne Boleyn for adultery (though the only adultery she ever committed was likely with Henry); mother of the future Queen Elizabeth.

Died — Jane Seymour; mother of the future King Edward VI.

Divorced — Anne of Cleves; the marriage was annulled after Henry saw her in person.

Executed — Catherine Howard for adultery; unlike Anne Boleyn, she did it.

Survived — Catherine Parr was probably more of a nurse for old, fat Henry. She has the distinction of being the only Queen of England to marry four times; twice a widow before marrying Henry, and then married after him.

2. One of Henry's favorite ways to eliminate people, including wives, was a bill of attainder. Stanford E. Lehmberg, *Parliamentary Attainder in the Reign of Henry VIII*, 18 Hist. J. 675, 688 (1975). Attainders were bills in Parliament for the specific purpose of finding persons guilty outside the normal criminal process under the common law. Henry did not invent them; during the War of the Roses, whatever side got power would commonly attaint the other side. Lehmberg at 676.

Henry did not use attainder for the first fifteen years of his reign, until he broke with Rome. *Id.* at 677, 681. Later, he attainted 130 persons: 96 for treason, 26 for misprision, 5 for felony, and 3 for heresy. *Id.* at 701; *see also* Kynell at 176 (on Henry using attainder to do away with habeas corpus).

Attainder extinguished a person's civil rights, making him dead civilly. For this reason, it was totally contrary to the foundation of America, that everyone has "*inalienable*" rights. *See* The Federalist No. 44 (James Madison). For this reason, the Constitution prohibits bills of attainder in three different places: "*No Bill of Attainder . . . shall be passed,*" U.S. Const. art. I, § 9, cl. 3; "*No State shall . . . pass any Bill of Attainder . . . ,*" U.S. Const. art. I, § 10, cl. 1; "*The Congress shall have Power to declare the Punishment of Treason, but no Attainder of Treason shall work Corruption of Blood, or Forfeiture except during the Life of the Person attainted,*" U.S. Const. art. III, § 3, cl. 2. Regarding attainders and the Constitution, see Jacob Reynolds, *The Rule of Law and the Origins of the Bill of Attainder Clause*, 18 St. Thomas L. Rev. 177, 194–97 (2005).

3. Among other methods, Henry controlled the press to advance his "*lust and thrust by greed.*" Kynell at 181.

4. As historian Colin Lovell puts it, "*the mass of men . . . accepted the Tudor idea that all things were now Caesar's.*" Lovell at 270.

5. Levy, Fifth Amendment, at 94. For a history of More, see the brief biography by his son-in-law, William Roper. Roper; *see also Saint Thomas More,* The Catholic Encyclopedia, http://www.newadvent.org/cathen/14689c.htm (last visited Aug. 22, 2005). *See generally* (among several biographies) Richard Marius, Thomas More: A Biography (1985); Peter Ackroyd, The Life of Thomas More (1999). For a less flattering view of More, from the Protestant perspective, see Michael Farris, From Tyndale to Madison: How the Death of an English Martyr Led to the American Bill of Rights ch. 3 (2007).

Sir Thomas More

Making his persecution particularly ironic was that More was *"silent"* on the whole matter. He had retreated from public life citing *"ill health"* after only three years as chancellor.[6] More was, however, writing a great deal at this time in support of the Church of Rome. Although he did not directly attack his old friend King Henry, the message was clear.

More was *"a man for all seasons"* as his friend Erasmus called him, a great light of humanist thinking not only in England but throughout Europe. More's book UTOPIA was an international best seller and a great book of western literature.[7]

To More's house sojourned some of the greatest

literary men of the age, including Erasmus.[8] It was while visiting More in 1509 that Erasmus wrote IN PRAISE OF FOLLY, a satirical essay that is one of the most notable works of the Renaissance and, though neither Erasmus nor More intended it, a catalyst of the Protestant Reformation.[9]

---

6. The Lord Chancellor—now the Lord High Chancellor of Great Britain—is still one of the most important officers in British government. Today the sovereign appoints him on the prime minister's advice. He is Speaker of the House of Lords, participates in the cabinet, acts as the custodian of the great seal, and heads the judiciary.

Thus, he has executive, legislative, and judicial powers. The British have limited the office in modern times. *See* Diana Woodhouse, *United Kingdom: The Constitutional Reform Act 2005— Defending Judicial*

The lord chancellor

Independence the English Way, 5 INT'L J. CONST. L. 153 (2007); Susanna Frederick Fischer, *Playing Poohsticks with the British Constitution: The Blair Government's Proposal to Abolish the Lord Chancellor*, 24 PENN. ST. INT'L L. REV. 257 (2005).

Originally chancellors were clergy and the king's chaplain/confessor and thus *"keeper of the king's conscience."* They began to provide direct justice, dispensing with legal technicalities, later called the "law of equity." Because the chancellor used to be the king's confessor or chaplain, he thus worked behind the screen or *cancelli*, which is where the word "chancellor" originates. LOVELL at 90. In England, the office goes at least as far back as the Norman Conquest of 1066.

Because usually only clerics could read during most of the Middle Ages, the lord chancellor was almost always a cleric. At this point, only the king's justiciar—essentially the viceroy for the absent Norman kings—outranked him, but when the justiciar office ended, only the king outranked the Chancellor.

The Lord Chancellor attended the *curia regis* (royal court), which evolved into Parliament. The Chancellor's judicial duties also evolved through the *curia regis*, and the High Court of Chancery developed to decide cases according to fairness or "equity" instead of the strict common law. Clergy dominated the chancellorship until 1529, after Cardinal Wolsey's dismissal.

---

7. Thomas More's UTOPIA (1516) (the full title of which is OF THE BEST STATE OF A REPUBLIC, AND OF THE NEW ISLAND UTOPIA or, in Latin, LIBELLUS VERE AUREUS, NEC MINUS SALUTARIS QUAM FESTIVUS, DE OPTIMO REI PUBLICAE *Statu deque* NOVA INSULA *Utopia)* describes More's fictional Atlantic island that is the site of a seemingly perfect society. The work presents More's social ideas, which stand up even today:

"For if you suffer your people to be ill-educated, and their manners to be corrupted from their infancy, and then punish them for those crimes to which their first education disposed them, what else is to be concluded from this, but that you first make thieves and then punish them." MORE, UTOPIA, Book 1.

Drew Barrymore's character, Cinderella, quotes this

passage in EVER AFTER: A CINDERELLA STORY (20th Century Fox 1998).

UTOPIA is also social satire. More got the name "utopia" from the Greek: "οὐ," ("not") and "τόπος," ("place"), literally "no place." Thus, Utopia is either a place of perfection or nonexistence.

An imagining of More's island, Utopia

8. Both of these Erasmus portraits show books; he embraced the press just as we embrace a new laptop computer. Erasmus translated the Greek Bible, which Martin

Luther used to translate the Bible into German. Thus, Erasmus, a Catholic and Luther detractor, contributed to the Protestant Reformation.

9. Both Erasmus and More had translated the Greek satirist Lucian into Latin, and both Erasmus's IN PRAISE OF FOLLY and More's UTOPIA show this influence. Both works share a dry humor with double or triple meanings throughout. For example, the title of Erasmus's work in Greek, *Moriae Enkomiom,* can also mean "In Praise of More." The essay starts as virtuoso foolery but then takes a darker tone in a series of orations, as Folly praises self-deception and madness and moves to a satirical examination of pious but superstitious abuses of Catholic doctrine and corrupt practices in parts of the Roman Catholic Church. Erasmus meant it to help the Catholic Church reform, but it also encouraged the Protestant Reformation.

The More household praised books and learning.[1] In today's parlance, we would describe More as "tied in" to the "new information highway" and the "worldwide web" of learning and culture. As noted, printing changed everything, just as the computer has changed everything for us.

In the case of heretical speech, More was constrictive.[2] But when it came to freely speaking political ideas and thoughts, he was expansive. As speaker of the House of Commons, he supported the relatively new idea that all members should speak freely and even criticize the king's policies.

In his PETITION FOR PARLIAMENTARY FREE SPEECH, More argued to Henry that if Parliament was to be of counsel to the king, the members needed to speak freely. Only this, pleaded More, would ensure the king the best advice possible.[3]

This was the first petition ever made in Parliament for free speech[4] and thus a precursor to the First Amendment.[5]

Unfortunately for More, it was his prominence as a man of speech and letters that made his silence so loud. For one thing, in the 1500s a king's servant did not simply resign. A minister such as Thomas More served at the King's pleasure. Thus, More's public resignation for *"ill health"* was a statement of his disagreement with Henry.

---

1. We have Hans Holbein's sketch of the More family portrait of 1527 but unfortunately fire destroyed the original painting. Reproduced here is one of two copies of Holbein's original. It shows a family that reads. Nearly everyone, including the women, hold books.

2. More was always concerned that *"the stretys were lykely to swarme full of heretykes."* THOMAS MORE, APOLOGY OF SYR THOMAS MORE KNIGHT, 219a-227b (1533), *quoted in* LEVY, FIFTH AMENDMENT, at 65.

3. We have More's PETITION FOR FREE SPEECH from William Roper and confirmed in Parliament's records. Excerpts from a modernized version show an interesting insight into human behavior: *"There can be no doubt that the assembly is a very substantial one, of very wise and politic persons. And yet, most victorious Prince, among so many wise men, not all will be equally wise, and of those who are equally wise, not all will be equally well-spoken. And often it happens that just as a lot of foolishness is uttered with ornate and polished speech, so, too, many coarse and rough-spoken men see deep indeed and give very substantial counsel."*

With this in mind More, always a lawyer, pleads that *"many of your discreet commoners will be hindered from giving their advice and counsel, to the great hindrance of the common affairs, unless every one of your commoners is utterly discharged of all doubt and fear as to how anything that* he happens to say may happen to be taken by your Highness." Accordingly, Henry should *"remove the misgivings of their timorous minds and animate and encourage and reassure them."* Also, Henry should *"give to all your commoners here assembled your most gracious permission and allowance for every man freely, without fear of your dreaded displeasure, to speak his conscience and boldly declare his advice concerning everything that comes up among us . . . ."*

For a complete text of this petition, see Center for Thomas More Studies, http://www.thomasmorestudies. org/segn/control/context?docId=2&searchDocId=2&selectedDoc=2&offset=0&version=modern& xpath=/wp:Document/wp:Content/page[1]&allDoc=true (last visited Aug. 12, 2010). Regarding More and Parliamentary free speech, see LOVELL at 240.

More's signature

Henry sent Thomas Cromwell to actively induce More to publicly endorse the king as head of the church— or to kill More.[6]

Specifically, Cromwell made More publicly refuse to swear to the Act of Supremacy of 1534. This act had an added clause repudiating *"any foreign authority, prince or potentate,"* an obvious reference to the Pope. By its terms, anyone who was called upon had to take an oath supporting the act.

More asserted himself *"a faithful subject of the King."* This, however, was far less than the age demanded, and Cromwell sent him to the Tower of London, the monarch's special prison for political opponents.[7]

More stayed there until a "special commission" indicted him for high treason. He was tried in July 1535.[8]

Much of the trial involved Cromwell trying to get More to confess that the Act

of Supremacy was illegal. By so doing, More would have committed treason.

During his persecution More never compromised on his understanding of the difference between the law of God and the law of the realm, which *"was the difference between heaven and hell."* In this he follows Saint Augustine regarding the "city of man" versus the "city of God" and is also a precursor of ideas of separation of church and state.

---

4. G.R. Elton, The Tudor Constitution: Documents and Commentary 255 (1960).

5. The U.S. Constitution specifically enshrines the concept of parliamentary free speech, providing *"for any Speech or Debate in either House, [a senator or representative] shall not be questioned in any other Place."* U.S. Const. art I, § 6.

Cromwell

6. Cromwell and More had a collegial relationship, but Cromwell knew his job was to please a fickle Henry. Also, Cromwell, unlike the essentially Catholic Henry, was what we would call a Lutheran.

7. Cromwell's specific authority came from the fact that Henry made Cromwell his vice regent and authorized him in 1535 to exercise all ecclesiastical jurisdictions with a "special commission." Cromwell's commission expired with his execution in 1540. Henry's daughter, Queen Mary Tudor, however, liked the idea of "commissions" to root out heresy. This eventually led to the infamous Court of High Commission. See Levy, Fifth Amendment, at 76.

8. More's judicial murder was typically Tudor. Henry VIII's father, Henry VII, started the Tudor dynasty with an indirect claim to the throne supported by various legal arguments. Thus, the Tudors were always keen to use "legal" procedures to achieve their ends, which included a lot of judicial murder.

In A Man for All Seasons Paul Scofield won an Oscar for his portrayal of More. Screenwriter Robert Bolt presented well the issues that led More to the block. It is still common even today to see More's life invoked, especially in legal circles. See, e.g., Blake D. Morant, *Lessons from Thomas More's Dilemma of Conscience: Reconciling the Clash Between a Lawyer's Beliefs and Professional Expectations*, 78 St. John's L. Rev. 965 (2004).

The Tower of London

More did not confess. Instead, Cromwell found a perjurer in the person of Richard Rich, the solicitor general.[1] Rich testified that in a conversation in the Tower, More had denied Parliament's power to confer ecclesiastical supremacy on Henry and that More had said something to the effect that Parliament could not pass a law that *"God was not God."*[2]

Though More denounced Rich as a perjurer, Cromwell's picked jury sealed More's fate. He was condemned and beheaded within the week.[3] But what he lived and died for eventually became part of the First Amendment's foundation.

HENRY'S PROGENY: EDWARD, MARY, AND ELIZABETH TUDOR

Henry VIII died in 1547, and the young and sickly Edward VI took over. He, or his regents, abolished all of Henry's treason and heresy laws—a promising start.[4]

But six years later, in 1553, Edward died, and his half-

Richard Rich

1. Rich had to resign as solicitor general to testify, but Cromwell made it worthwhile for him. Today's lawyers have MODEL RULE OF PROFESSIONAL CONDUCT 3.7, which directs that *"[a] lawyer shall not act as advocate at a trial in which the lawyer is likely to be a necessary witness . . ."* Rich was an ambitious and shrewd man, as shadowy as the Holbein sketch of him. Five years later he had a hand in Cromwell's execution. Rich died in his bed a wealthy old man.

2. For More's trial as it relates to the history of the right to remain silent, *see* **Chapter 5 of** *Bills, Quills, and Stills,* **(Constitution Press re-release 2017).**

3. More was to be hanged, drawn, and quartered, but Henry "commuted" his sentence to beheading and, as was customary, his head was parboiled and put on the pole on London Bridge. More's daughter, Margaret, bribed the Bridge watchman and got the head for burial so that it would not be thrown into the Thames river. Henry's commutation was actually something of a kindness, in that hanging involved being cut down while still alive, and then having your genitalia cut off and your "entrails" dissected and burnt in front of you (they seemed to be good at keeping you alive for this), finally having your head cut off and your body quartered and dispersed to the four corners of the realm after the executioner cut out your heart and held it up for public view. BLACK'S LAW DICTIONARY 645 (5th ed. 1979). Also *see* BRAVEHEART (20th Century Fox 1995) for a simulation—not too gory—of the procedure. *See* **Chapter 8 of** *Bills, Quills, and Stills,* **(Constitution Press re-release 2017).**

Margaret More

Site of More's execution on the Tower of London grounds

4. During the six years of his reign only two heretics burned. In contrast, during four years of Mary's reign 273 burned.

Edward VI was also "the Prince" in Mark Twain's THE PRINCE AND THE PAUPER (1882), about a young prince being mistaken for a common boy who looks just like him. Twain's story has been adapted numerous times including *The Prince and the Pauper* (Classic Comics, Issue 29 1946) as well as film and television versions, including THE PRINCE AND THE PAUPER (1937), starring Errol Flynn, and a Disney short film THE PRINCE AND THE PAUPER (Buena Vista Pictures 1990), starring Mickey Mouse in a critically acclaimed dramatic performance.

Edward VI

sister, Mary, took over.[5] This daughter of Catherine of Aragon believed it her mission to take England back to the Catholic Church. What you believed and said about it again became a crime.[6]

Mary took a page from Henry's book and established a commission "*for a severer way of proceeding against heretics*."[7] Mary's commission eventually became the Court of High Commission, which was the ecclesiastical arm of the Privy Council, just as the Star Chamber was the judicial arm.

Under Henry, all ecclesiastical power came under the sovereign, not from a pesky archbishop or pope. Despite her Catholicity, Mary saw no need to change this particular power structure.

But despite Mary's best efforts, English Protestantism lived on. After her death in 1558, Mary's half-sister (the daughter of Anne Boleyn) Elizabeth I took over. Elizabeth repealed all Mary's legislation against heresy.[8] Elizabeth was personally a moderate in an intolerant age.[9]

Mary Tudor

5. LEVY, FIFTH AMENDMENT at 75 (quoting the Catholic historian Philip Hughes that "*[t]he facts are that in the last four years of Mary's reign, between February 4, 1555, and November 10, 1558, something like 273 of her subjects were executed by burning, under laws that her government had revived for the capital crime of obstinately adhering to beliefs that contradicted the teaching of the Catholic Church . . . . In this respect alone, namely of so many executions for this particular offence in so short a time, the event is a thing apart, in English history: never before, nor ever since, was there anything at all quite like it.*").

The work of Mary's Commission and its 273 victims earned her the title Bloody Mary. *Id.* at 76–77.

Turning to a less grave historical point, Mary's historical nickname raises the question of whether the Bloody Mary cocktail was named after her. It is a mixture in varying proportions of tomato juice, vodka, and other flavorings such as Worcestershire and/or Tabasco sauce. If the drink was named for her, she certainly never had one. Mary died in 1558, and tomatoes and potatoes (the latter for the vodka) did not make it to England until the 1590s. Other variations of the Bloody Mary with alternate ingredients include the Bloody Maria, with tequila; Bloody Geisha, with sake; Red Snapper, with gin; Michelada, with beer; Bullshot, with beef bouillon instead of tomato juice; Caesar or Bloody Caesar, with Clamato; and the Virgin Mary, Bloody Virgin, or A Bloody Shame, all with no alcohol.

6. Given that publishing at this point was mostly about religion, Mary renewed the old punishment for libelous printers: amputating a hand. Her first victim was a publisher aptly named John Stubbes. SADAKAT KADRI, THE TRIAL: A HISTORY, FROM SOCRATES TO O.J. SIMPSON 76 (2005).

7. One of these heretics who met his fate under Mary was Archbishop of Canterbury **Thomas Cranmer**. Granting the divorce of Mary's dad from her mom turned out to be a bad career move.

Cranmer burned as a heretic from FOXE'S BOOK OF MARTYRS

8. She was called Good Queen Bess, Gloriana, and, because she never married, the Virgin Queen. Nobody believes she was a virgin, but the state of Virginia is named after her. Of course, if she really was a virgin, it would cut against the slogan "*Virginia is for Lovers.*"

9. During her reign only four Anabaptists burned. At the time, all the major factions of Christendom agreed that Anabaptists were heretics. Anabaptists denied the validity of infant baptism and, therefore, practiced rebaptism for adults. The movement was prominent during the sixteenth century and lives on in the Mennonite religion. The Baptists later adopted Anabaptist teaching regarding infant baptism. *See Anabaptists*, THE CATHOLIC ENCYCLOPEDIA, http://www.newadvent.org/cathen/01445b.htm (last visited Aug. 29, 2005).

But relying on this view of Elizabeth misses a subtlety about her reign. More than even under Henry, religious nonconformity became treason; her government was zealous in ferreting it out, sending scores to prison, torture, and the gallows.[1]

Much of this resulted from Elizabeth's weak position when she took the throne. Besides the problem of being Anne Boleyn's daughter, Elizabeth was still illegitimate under both canon law and statute when she became queen. She even had trouble finding a bishop to perform the coronation.[2]

Plus, Elizabeth had the unique problem of being a female sovereign. With the Acts of Supremacy and Uniformity, she reestablished Henry's break with Rome, but, unlike dad, she could not be the church's "supreme head." No Protestant reform of that age went so far as to accept a woman priest, thus precluding Elizabeth from becoming the Pope of England.[3] Instead, she became the church's "supreme governor"— certainly good enough for her ends.

Pope Pius V convicted her of heresy in 1570 (*in absentia*, of course) and excommunicated her. The papal bull[4] that followed deposed her as queen, absolved her subjects

---

1. Sir Francis Walsingham (c. 1530–90) was Elizabeth's "spymaster." He admired Machiavelli, as can be seen in his quote

"*[t]here is less danger in fearing too much than too little,*" and was one of the most proficient espionage-weavers in history. His intelligence on the Spanish Armada contributed to its defeat, and he discovered the plots around Mary, Queen of Scots, and actively participated in the trial leading to her execution. Even the playwright Christopher Marlowe was one of his spies. The modern British spy services, MI5 and MI6, have their origins in Walsingham's networks. Without Walsingham there would be no James Bond or George Smiley. *See generally* ALAN HAYNES, INVISIBLE POWER: THE ELIZABETHAN SECRET SERVICES 1570–1603 (1992).

James Bond, or 007 (pronounced "double oh seven"), is a fictional British spy created by writer Ian Fleming in 1953. So far, six actors have played Bond in the official series: Sean Connery, George Lazenby , Roger Moore, Timothy Dalton, Pierce Brosnan, and, since 2006, Daniel Craig.

George Smiley is John Le Carré's fictional MI6 agent and the central character in the novels CALL FOR THE DEAD (1961); A MURDER OF QUALITY (1962); TINKER, TAILOR, SOLDIER, SPY (1974); THE HONOURABLE SCHOOLBOY (1977); and SMILEY'S PEOPLE (1979). Alec Guinness played him in two successful television adaptations. Smiley is stodgy and ponderous and thus the antithesis of Bond.

2. Elizabeth I's coronation painting (1559).

Sean Connery as Bond

3. LEVY, FIFTH AMENDMENT, at 85. The movie ELIZABETH (Gramercy 1998) depicts many of the issues facing the queen, including the religious tensions between Catholic and Anglican prelates. Though a historian could quibble with details and event timing, the movie presents the issues with great performances by Cate Blanchard as Elizabeth and Geoffrey Rush as Walsingham.

Daniel Craig also plays an assassin Jesuit "hit man," based on John Ballard, a Jesuit priest executed in 1586 for plotting to kill Elizabeth. Craig later brought that assassin quality to his James Bond role in CASINO ROYALE (Columbia Pictures 2006).

4. A papal bull is a special pronuncment by a pope and named for the lead seal (bulla) authenticating it.

Pope Pius V and Elizabeth

Papal bull (Pope Urban VIII, 1637) sealed with a leaden *bulla*

5. LEVY, FIFTH AMENDMENT, at 88. The Bull of Deposition, *Regnans in Excelsis* ("Ruling from on High") marked a turn in Elizabeth's policy of religious toleration, and she began to persecute her religious enemies after it.

The bull's relevant section reads as follows:

"*And moreover We do declare her to be deprived of her pretended title to the kingdom aforesaid, and of all dominion, dignity, and privilege whatsoever; and also the nobility, subjects, and people of the said kingdom, and all others who have in any sort sworn unto her, to be for ever absolved from any such oath, and all manner of duty dominion, allegiance, and obedience; and . . . We do command and charge all and every the noblemen, subjects, people, and others aforesaid that they presume not to obey her or her orders, mandates, and laws; and those which shall do the contrary. We do include them in the like sentence of anathema . . . .*"

Quoted in LEVY, FIFTH AMENDMENT, at 454 n.5.

from obeying her, and, for good measure, excommunicated any who did.[5]

This made it dicey to be Catholic in England. It became high treason in 1559 just to say that Elizabeth was not queen and in 1571 to allege she was a heretic or schismatic. Her government imposed crushing fines on Catholics, closed Catholic seminaries, and executed priests, especially Jesuits.[6]

And yet the priests still came, often hidden by Catholics.[7] When they were found, though, the charge was not heresy but treason.[8]

All of this underscores the problem with an "established" religion: heresy, a belief outside the official religious norm or orthodoxy, becomes treason. This is exactly why the Framers of the Constitution wrote the First Amendment's Establishment Clause.

But Catholics were not Elizabeth's only problem; there were also the Puritans. Initially, Elizabeth's government gave them a pass because they counterbalanced the Catholics. But as the Catholic threat diminished, especially with the defeat of the Spanish Armada in 1588, things changed.[9] The queen, like her father, was personally conservative in religion, with no affinity for Puritan radicalism.[10]

---

6. In 1585 Parliament banished all Catholic priests as traitors with An Act Against Jesuits, Seminary Priests and Such Other Like Disobedient Persons. Elizabeth executed 200 Catholics for "treason," all the while maintaining that it was not because they were Catholic. Lovell at 267.

7. Many were hidden in "priest holes," hiding places for priests built into many Roman Catholic houses of England, especially during Elizabeth's reign. Most are attributed to the Jesuit Nicholas Owen, who constructed them to protect persecuted Roman Catholic priests.

Concealed priest hole in Partingdale House, Middlesex

R P Edmundus Campianus Soc IF Sac

8. See generally Levy, Fifth Amendment, ch. 3. English Catholic priests came back to England after training in special seminaries abroad and presented a threat to Elizabeth's government. For this, she had them killed. One was Jesuit Father Edmund Campion, executed in 1581 after a sham trial. For Campion's trial in the context of the right to remain silent, see **Chapter 5 of Bills, Quills, and Stills, (Constitution Press re-release 2017).**

9. Elizabeth in 1588, showing the defeat of the Spanish Armada in the background.

10. Starting in 1563, John Foxe published his Book of Martyrs, giving accounts of the religious persecutions and Protestant martyrs. For over a century only the Bible was more popular in England than Foxe's Book of Martyrs. It became a primer on the values of freedom of religion and speech, at least from the Protestant perspective. See Levy, Fifth Amendment, at 79–82. The book's full title begins with Actes and Monuments of these Latter and Perillous Days, Touching Matters of the Church. Through many editions, it became the affirmation of the Protestant Reformation in England. Foxe wanted to show the Church of England's historical foundation as the true and faithful church over Roman Catholicism. Foxe's record is extremely partisan and became the primary propaganda piece for English anti-Catholicism. Among other objections, Foxe's claims regarding martyrdoms under Mary ignore the mingled political and religious aspects of the time.

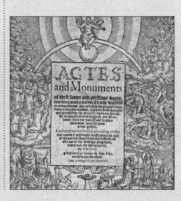

Leaving aside Elizabeth's religiosity, the issue was power. Elizabeth believed the state should control the church to effect her secular ends. The Puritans believed the church should control the state to affect heaven on earth. Here converges the Puritan and Catholic notion of the relationship between church and state. Both agreed that the church should control; they just had different notions of "the church."[1]

In Elizabeth's day, there were no grand political parties or movements. People instead articulated their politics through religion.

Among Elizabeth's tools of power were licensing and censorship, which her government employed more broadly than ever. In the early days of Henry VIII, printing and debate were much more open.[2] With the Elizabethan

settlement in 1559 began a system that required government licenses to speak or print.

Elizabeth's successor, James I, expanded the licensing to support his established church.[3] Religion and speech are locked in history, which explains why the Framers put them together in the First Amendment.

Elizabeth in 1575

1. Elizabeth saw the matter very clearly when stating that Catholics and Puritans *"join together in one opinion against me, for neither of them would have me to be Queen of England."* Quoted in LEVY, FIFTH AMENDMENT, at 147.

2. Elizabeth was no fan of parliamentary free speech, as Thomas More had advocated in the early days of Henry VIII.

For one thing, Parliament did not know the reason she called it until her opening speech, and it was to follow her agenda. LOVELL at 233. In 1592, she advised the Speaker of the House of Commons that free speech was *"not as some suppose to speak . . . of all causes as him listeth, and to frame a form of religion, or a state of Government as to their idle brains shall seem meetest. She sayeth no king for his state will suffer such absurdities."* Quoted in id. at 233.

The speaker of the House was a royal nominee to forward her agenda, and she severely treated speakers who failed her. Id. at 237. Ultimately, she could veto anything Parliament did. Id. at 238.

3. See Witte, *Milton*, at 1588, *citing* CYNTHIA SUSAN CLEGG, PRESS CENSORSHIP IN ELIZABETHAN ENGLAND (1997); CYNTHIA SUSAN CLEGG, CENSORSHIP IN JACOBEAN ENGLAND (2001); DAVID LOADES, POLITICS, CENSORSHIP AND THE ENGLISH REFORMATION (1991); S. MUTCHOW TOWERS, CONTROL OF RELIGIOUS PRINTING IN EARLY STUART ENGLAND (2003).

THE STUARTS

The Stuarts seem out of place.

Coming from Scotland may have had something to do with it. But they were not just out of place, they were out of sync; eventually, they were out of time.[4]

James I followed the popular Elizabeth in 1603. His son Charles I became king in 1625 but got his head chopped off in 1649. After Cromwell's "protectorate," Charles II took over in 1660 and tried to implement a French-style absolute monarchy but without the resources to make it work. When his less capable brother James II took over in 1685, he tried to do the same and lost the throne in 1688.

Although this book is not a history of the Stuarts, their story plays out over several chapters as it relates to the Bill of Rights. Religion and free speech especially bedeviled them.

James I: James I was a big advocate of the divine right of kings—being one, it came easily to him. In 1598, he wrote THE TRUE LAW OF FREE MONARCHIES, asserting among other things, "*rex est loquens*," ("the king is the law speaking").[5] James was an educated man and technically he was not saying he was above the law but that he embodied the law!

---

4. James I, king of England, was also James VI of Scotland and the son of Mary, Queen of Scots. Elizabeth had had Mary beheaded for treason. But in an historical irony, Mary's son James followed Elizabeth as king of England. Then followed Charles I, but Parliament deposed him, which led to Oliver Cromwell becoming "lord protector" (i.e., dictator) of England. Shortly after Cromwell's death, Charles II was "restored" to the throne, followed by James II. Finally, Mary (James II's Protestant daughter) ruled with her co-monarch husband, William of Orange.

William of Orange

Mary Stuart

5. *See* LEVY, FIFTH AMENDMENT, at 243.

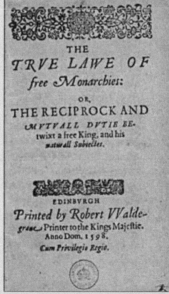

THE
TRVE LAWE OF
free Monarchies:

OR,

THE RECIPROCK AND
MVTVALL DVTIE BE-
twixt a free King, and his
naturall Subiectes.

EDINBVRGH
Printed by Robert Walde-
grave, Printer to the Kings Maiestie.
Anno Dom. 1598.
Cum Privilegio Regio.

THE TRUE LAW OF FREE MONARCHIES sets out the doctrine of the divine right of kings. James saw it as an extension of the apostolic succession, the practice whereby bishops consecrate new bishops and priests by laying hands on them. The practice traces back in an unbroken chain to the original twelve apostles. During the reign of James's son Charles I, in 1644 Samuel Rutherford wrote LEX, REX *(The Law Is King)*, expounding the theological arguments for the rule of law over the rule of men and kings.
  See SAMUEL RUTHERFORD, LEX, REX, *available at* Liberty Library of Constitutional Classics, http://www.constitution.org/sr/lexrex.htm (last visited Dec. 5, 2005).

Samuel Rutherford

Either way, according to James, only God could judge him.

In a speech to Parliament, for example, James asserted that kings are not just God's

"lieutenants upon earth, and sit upon God's throne, but even by God himselfe they are called Gods."[1]

This makes you wonder whether James was all that clear that even God would judge him!

As did the Tudors, James believed in an established religion declaring, *"No Bish-* *ops, no King,"* meaning that crown and church were intertwined. James supported the established church and it supported him.

And because bishops got their jobs from James, they really tried to ingratitate themselves to him. During one theological debate, the archbishop of Canterbury, John Whitgift, pronounced:

"Undoubtedly your majesty speaks by the special assistance of God's spirit."[2]

The bishop of London, Richard Bancroft, one-upped Whitgift, proclaiming,

"I protest my heart melteth with joy, that Almighty God, of his singular mercy, hath given us such a king, as, since Christ's time, the like hath not been."[3]

These guys were obviously practiced and talented suck-ups. No wonder that upon Whitgift's death in 1604, Bancroft got his job as archbishop of Canterbury. This put Bancroft in position to oversee the KING JAMES BIBLE, which he tailored to suit James, reworking passages to make it monarch-friendly.[4]

---

1. *Quoted in* LEVY, FIFTH AMENDMENT, at 207.

Even today the head of the Anglican Church—that is, the Church of England—is not the archbishop of Canterbury but the monarch, who as of this writing is Queen Elizabeth II.

2. LEVY, FIFTH AMENDMENT, at 212–13.

3. LEVY, FIFTH AMENDMENT, at 212–13.

Richard Bancroft   John Whitgift

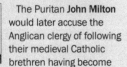

The Puritan **John Milton** would later accuse the Anglican clergy of following their medieval Catholic brethren having become

• "a tyrannical crew"
• a "corporation of imposters"
• "halting and time-serving" prelates

• "Egyptian taskmasters of ceremonies"
• "a heap of hard and loathsome uncleanness"
• a "whip of scorpions"
• "illiterate and blind guides"
• "a wasteful band of robbers"
• "a perpetual havoc and rapine"
• "a continual hydra of mischief and molestation"
• "importunate wolves"
• "wild boars"
• "locusts and scorpions"
• "downtrodden vassals of perdition"

Witte, *Milton*, at 1559.

Frontispiece to the KING JAMES BIBLE, 1611

4. The KING JAMES BIBLE is an English translation of the CHRISTIAN BIBLE begun in 1604 and completed in 1611. King James gave the translators instructions to guarantee that the new version would support both the Church of England and the monarchy. This was the third such official translation of the Bible into English, after THE GREAT BIBLE under Henry VIII and THE BISHOP'S BIBLE of 1568. All of these texts relied on William Tyndale's 1525 translation. Tyndale was the first to translate the Bible into English from Greek sources. He created new English words and expressions that we use even today, both in common speech and for their poetic value:

• "*Jehovah*" (from a transliterated Hebrew construction in the Old Testament, from "YHWH")
• "*Passover*" (as the name for the Jewish holiday "Pesach" or "Pesah")
• "*Atonement*" (at + onement), which goes beyond mere "reconciliation" to mean "to unite" or "to cover"
• "*scapegoat*" (the goat that bears the people's sins),
• "let there be light"
• "the powers that be"
• "my brother's keeper"
• "the salt of the earth"
• "a law unto themselves"
• "filthy lucre"
• "it came to pass"
• "gave up the ghost"
• "the signs of the times"
• "the spirit is willing"
• "live and move and have

Despite his arbitrary quirks, James would probably have had a relatively quiet reign but for the Puritans. To the Puritans, the religious power structures of the Tudors and Stuarts, like James's High Commission for Ecclesiastical Causes, represented the pope's law, and if there was one thing that a Puritan could not abide, it was "popery."[5]

What made matters worse for James was that these Puritans would not shut up.[6] James responded by trying to hinder speech itself. Indeed, James's restrictions on speech focused on both the religious and the political.

In 1621, James warned Parliament that it had no role in foreign affairs, saying it should not

"meddle with anything concerning our government or deep matters of state."[7]

Parliament, which by this point had become far more than the king's advisors with whom he could "parley," sent a protestation. James formally ripped the protestation out of the *Journals of the House.*

Edward Coke (pronounced "Cook"), later Lord Chief Justice of England, challenged James in a speech in the House of Commons. Members of Parliament, Coke declared, have an

"ancient right" and *"undoubted inheritance"* to a *"freedom to speak what we think good for government, either in church or commonwealth and what are the grievances . . . [T]he freedom of the House is the freedom of the whole land . . . . We serve here for thousands and ten thousands."*[8]

---

our being"
• "fight the good fight"
See MICHAEL FARRIS, FROM TYNDALE TO

Douai-Rheims New Testament

MADISON: HOW THE DEATH OF AN ENGLISH MARTYR LED TO THE AMERICAN BILL OF RIGHTS 23 (2007); TYNDALE'S NEW TESTAMENT (David Daniell ed., 1996). Many of these terms ended up in The KING JAMES BIBLE. The Catholic answer was THE DOUAY-RHEIMS BIBLE of 1582 (New Testament) and 1609–10 (Old Testament), which also borrowed from Tyndale.

William Tyndale burned in 1536 for translating the Bible into English

5. The Puritan John Milton, living in the aftermath of King James, wrote of the need to protect the individual's liberty of conscience and freedom of worship from what he called *"the greedy idols"* of established Anglicanism, the *"spiritual tyranny of idle ceremonies,"* *"corrosive customs,"* and *"erroneous beliefs."* Witte, *Milton,* at 1529.

6. For more on the Puritan legal battles with James's courts, see **Chapter 5 of Bills, Quills, and Stills, (Constitution Press re-release 2017).**

7. *Quoted in* Steve Bachmann, *Starting Again with the Mayflower . . . England's Civil War and America's Bill of Rights,* 20 QUINNIPIAC L. REV. 193, 216 (2000).

8. Witte, *Milton,* at 1588–89. Regarding James I's struggles with Parliament on free speech, including his jailing of Coke, see LOVELL at 303.

Sir Edward Coke

James did not want the *"thousands and ten thousands"* involved in politics either. James encouraged them to engage in traditional village sports on Sundays (the original "weekend warriors") to prevent them from wasting time in the alehouses talking sedition. Bachmann at 222.
You have to wonder whether the same things goes on today where men obsess about golf and the Super Bowl and repair to the modern sports bar only for buffalo wings, rather than dare talk politics.

Coke, like Sir Thomas More before him, was invoking a speech, petition, and debate tradition going back to the thirteenth century. Thus, when James I, and later Charles I, suspended Parliament and tried to curtail speech, Parliament indignantly rose up.[1]

These risings eventually killed James's son Charles I.

Charles I: As a modern commentator notes,

"[t]he most interesting thing about King Charles the First is that he was five feet six inches tall at the start of his reign, but only four foot eight inches tall at the end of it."[2]

In 1625, James's second son, Charles, took over and ruled until his head was chopped off in 1649. Like dad, he was a big fan of the divine right of kings, which led to a fruitless power struggle with Parliament.[3]

Charles was hapless,[4] but much of his problem was a changed world.

During the Middle Ages, the human condition limited the king's power. Even if the king was "divinely appointed," what did it really matter to his subjects? They probably never saw him or much of his government. If they had a legal dispute, for instance, they would seek justice from the local lord or church court, and only then voluntarily seek appeal to the king's common-law courts.[5]

But with the gradual development of modern taxing and bureaucracy, the monarch could directly or indirectly control everything. By Charles's time "divine right" was going out the door; people were starting to agree to government only if they had a stake in it and a voice about it.

John Lilburne

1. Coke's use of history became an important part of the English Revolution's ideology. John Lilburne used to go into the House of Commons during the 1640s with a Bible in one hand and Coke's law books, THE INSTITUTES, in the other. Harold J. Berman, *Law and Belief in Three Revolutions*, 18 VAL. U. L. REV. 569, 600 (1984).

2. "Oliver Cromwell," on *Monty Python Sings* (Virgin Records 1991), sung to the tune of Frederic Chopin's Polonaise Op. 53 in A Flat Major. Actually, Charles was 5'4."

4. As Levy comments, *"[i]f supreme political stupidity in a king merits his execution, Charles richly deserved his fate."* LEVY, FIFTH AMENDMENT, at 266. Lovell describes him as a *"kindly, obstinate, and rather stupid man . . . ."* LOVELL at 309.

5. For a discussion of English law in the middle ages see **Chapter 6 of Bills, Quills, and Stills,** (Constitution Press re-release 2017).

6. See Bachmann at 216–17; *see also* Witte, *Milton*, at 1532–36 (detailing the history of the English Civil War with Charles I).

7. *See* Harold W. Wolfram, *John Lilburne: Democracy's Pillar of Fire,* 3 SYRACUSE L. REV. 213, 220–21 and n.29 (1952).

The king summoned the **Long Parliament** in November 1640, so called to distinguish it from the **Short Parliament** he had summoned in April–May 1640. The Long Parliament also caused the king's advisers to resign and forbade its own dissolution without its members' consent. Tension between the king and Parliament increased until the English Civil War in 1642. After the king's defeat in 1646, the army exercised political power and in 1648 expelled all but sixty members of the Long Parliament. The remaining group, the **Rump Parliament**, brought Charles to trial and execution in 1649. It then stayed around until Cromwell forcibly ejected it in 1653.

Cromwell ejecting the Rump Parliament

3. Charles was compensating. He was Britain's shortest king. ANTONIA FRASER, THE LIVES OF THE KINGS AND QUEENS OF ENGLAND 181 (1975). His elder brother Henry was the heir apparent, but Henry died of typhoid in 1612.

Anthony van Dyck in this famous *Charles I, King of England, from Three Angles* (1636), masked Charles's small stature and also solved Charles's problem of deciding between his three favorite suits for the portrait.

Among the mistakes that led Charles to the chopping block were his struggles with Parliament in the 1620s. He fined and imprisoned members for speaking.[6] The Parliamentarians, especially the Puritans, pressed on, and Charles responded by dissolving Parliament.

Charles also tried to introduce a modified Anglican prayer book in Presbyterian Scotland, which led to a costly and unsuccessful war. His ineptitudes and financial need forced him to finally call a Parliament in 1640, after eleven years.[7]

This Long Parliament immediately sided with the Puritans, and in 1641, it abolished the courts in which Charles persecuted religious dissent and speech: the Court of High Commission for Ecclesiastical Causes and the Star Chamber.[8]

The Star Chamber in particular had been the court for prosecuting crimes such as counterfeiting and printing without a license.[9] Under the licensing laws, the bishop of London or archbishop of Canterbury reviewed all books, censored the illicit ones, and sent the unlicensed printers and authors to the Star Chamber for prosecution and punishment.[10]

When Parliament abolished the Star Chamber, the Tudor-Stuart licensing system became unenforceable, and the size of the press exploded.[11] For the first time, normal people could get their hands on cheap newspapers and political pamphlets.

A person's own voice limits the power of speech to those who can hear it or to those who "heard it said." The printed page, though, can literally go across all England and even across the ocean to colonial America.

---

8. The Star Chamber was particularly infamous among Puritans, many of whom came to America. *See Watts v. Indiana*, 338 U.S. 49, 54 (1949) ("*Ours is the accusatorial as opposed to the inquisitorial system. Such has been the characteristic of Anglo-American criminal justice since it freed itself from practices borrowed by the Star Chamber from the Continent whereby an accused was interrogated in secret for hours on end.*"). THE STAR CHAMBER (20th Century Fox 1983) uses the Star Chamber's historical infamy as a plot basis. Michael Douglas stars as a frustrated judge who joins a shadow court that hunts down "criminals" who "get off" because of legal technicalities. The movie works as a thriller, more or less, but relies on the tired (and false) premise that the criminal justice system is not convicting enough "bad guys."

9. To the English of the time, printing a book was like minting a coin. Indeed, the manufacturing process of producing the movable type for printing is similar to minting a coin. Without a license, the publication was presumed "counterfeit," and printing, selling, or possessing it was an actionable crime. Witte, *Milton*, at 1589–90.

10. The Stationers' Company, the monopoly that enforced the licensing law, could "*search what houses and shops (and at what time they shall think fit)*" for illegal publications. Witte, *Milton*, at 1589–90. Regarding the history of search and seizure, see **Chapter 4 of *Bills, Quills, and Stills*, (Constitution Press re-release 2017).**

11. By one count, the number of pamphlets published during the year 1640 was 22, but by 1642 it was 1,966. Witte, *Milton*, at 1589; *see also* Bachmann at 220.

For centuries, kings had licensed and censured printing with varying degrees of success.[1] Now, who could turn back the tide of free speech?[2]

An alarmed Parliament tried to do so in June 14, 1643, by issuing a new licensing law to stamp out the "*many false, forged, scandalous, seditious, libelous, and unlicensed Papers, Pamphlets, and Books to the great defamation of Religion and government*."[3] A dozen Protestant ministers replaced the bishop of London as censor and Parliament replaced the Star Chamber as enforcer.

But "free expression" had become its own political end, not just a way to get religious freedom or other rights. Thus, it deserved its own defense. The Puritan poet John Milton rose to the challenge with the masterful AREOPAGITICA (1644).[4]

By 1642, the English Civil War had begun. Parliament eventually defeated the royalist forces for good in 1648. Kings had been deposed before, but Parliament specifically tried Charles

1. Official censorship in England started before the Tudors, in 1275, with *De Scandalis Magnatum* for "seditious words" about the king or his officials. O'Brien at 43. But the printing press of the mid-1400s and Henry VIII's break with Rome made the practice a royal imperative. Henry VIII had a licensing law in 1530. The later Tudors and Stuarts broadened it with a dozen later acts, culminating in Charles I's Star Chamber Decree of 1637. Witte, *Milton*, at 1589–90.

2. Even today dictatorial regimes bring to bear all the resources of modern police technology against the expression of free speech and democracy. So far, they have all eventually failed as the fall of the Berlin Wall showed. But they often only fail after much human misery, and many have yet to do so, as the Tiananmen Square protests of 1989 showed.

Berlin Wall at the Brandenburg Gate, November 9, 1989

3. *Quoted in* Witte, *Milton*, at 1589–90.

"Tank man" was an anonymous man who blocked Chinese tanks on June 5, 1989, after the Chinese removed protestors from Tiananmen Square
Image by Helen Koop

William Blake's version of John Milton

4. John Milton (1604–74) wrote during the throes of the English Revolution, 1640–60. His PARADISE LOST (1667–68) is a masterpiece of English literature. In AREOPAGITICA: A SPEECH OF MR. JOHN MILTON FOR THE LIBERTY OF UNLICENSED PRINTING TO THE PARLIAMENT OF ENGLAND (1644), he defended freedom of expression:

- a nation's unity is created through blending individual differences rather than imposing homogeneity;
- the ability to explore the fullest range of ideas on a given issue is essential to find truth;
- censorship acts to the detriment of material progress;
- if the facts are laid bare, truth will defeat falsehood in open competition, but this cannot be left for a single individual to determine: "*Let her and Falsehood grapple; who ever knew Truth put to the worse in a free and open encounter?*";
- each individual must uncover his own truth because no one is wise enough to act as a censor for all individuals: "*Each person has the law of God written on his and her heart, mind, and conscience, and rewritten in Scripture, most notably in the Decalogue.*"

Quoted in Witte, *Milton*, at 1529, 1586.

Regarding Milton's influence on America and the First Amendment, John Adams wrote in 1776 that Milton was "*as honest a man as his nation ever bred, and as great a friend of liberty.*"

for high treason.[5] Charles refused to enter a plea, claiming that no court had jurisdiction over a monarch and that the court's power was nothing more than what grew out of a barrel of gunpowder. This sealed his fate.

As Milton noted, England was ready to embrace democracy. Give people education and

"all the Lord's people . . . become prophets . . . [T]he right of choosing, yea of changing their own government is by the grant of God himself in the people."[6]

Poor Charles never "got it." He, too, wanted the people's liberty,

"but I must tell you," declared Charles, *"that their Liberty and Freedom consist in*

having government . . . . It is not their having a share in the government—that is nothing appertaining to them."[7]

From his scaffold, Charles I looked over a changed world; how much insight he had into the change is impossible to know because they chopped his head off before he could say.[8]

First page of the 1644 edition of Areopagitica. The title "Areopagitica" alludes to an analogous written oration of Isocrates presented in 355 BC to the Athenian Ecclesia, advocating a return of certain powers to the aristocratic Council of the Areopagus.

The Temptation and Fall of Eve by William Blake (1808), from Paradise Lost

Title page of the first edition of *Paradise Lost*, 1668

Paradise Lost has been just too good for Hollywood to pass up. Seven (New Line Cinema 1995) includes quotations from the poem; The Devil's Advocate (Warner Brothers 1997) alludes to it and includes the line "better to reign in Hell, than serve in Heaven," and Al Pacino's Satan is named "John Milton." (The "devil's advocate" was originally a canon lawyer in the Roman Catholic Church appointed to argue against a person's canonization or beatification. Pope Sixtus V institutionalized the office in 1587. Kadri at 146.) The Crow (Miramax Films 1989) quotes from the poem, as does The Prophecy (Dimension Films 1995) and The Sentinel (Universal Pictures 1977).

5. Trial of Charles I.

6. *Quoted in* Witte, *Milton*, at 1596, 1598.

7. *Quoted in* Wolfram at 227. Bachmann at 195–96 gives Charles's fuller quote from the scaffold: *"For the people . . . truly I desire their liberty and freedom as much as anybody whatsoever; but I must tell you, their liberty and freedom consists in having government, those laws by which their lives and their goods may be most their own. It is not their having a share in the government; that is nothing appertaining to them. A subject and a sovereign are clear different things."*

8. Execution of Charles I (contemporary German print).

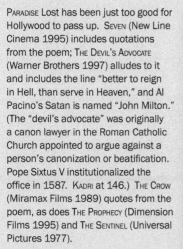

Petitioning Cromwell for Everything: Charles was gone. A nice story would be that his demise ushered in an era of toleration, rights, and freedom that transplanted to America. Unfortunately, this was not the case.

Oliver Cromwell eventually emerged as the military dictator of England from 1649 until his death in 1658.[1] This was an unprecedented time of petitions, including THE HUMBLE PETITION OF THE LEVELERS (1647), AN AGREEMENT OF THE PEOPLE (1647), and THE HUMBLE PETITION AND ADVICE (1657).

The power in these petitions lay not so much that they were printed but in the process by which they came about. Large groups produced them, which showed political power. They were symbols as much as proposals.[2]

Cromwell generally ignored the petitions and famously put the greatest petitioner of all, John Lilburne, on trial.[3] But the power of petitions and the way in which they could marshal people and politics is exactly what the First Amendment guarantees. It is no accident that the Framers put the right to "*assemble*" and "*petition*" in the same clause.[4]

Restoration of Charles II: The Puritan Revolution, which had devolved into Cromwell's Protectorate, ended with the Stuart Restoration.[5]

In an historical inversion, Charles II was

1. Cromwell in his famous "warts and all" painting. Cromwell wanted this painting to distinguish himself from the way monarchs had themselves painted, most notably Charles I's flattering portraits to increase his stature.

Cromwell turned out to be as despotic as a king—perhaps more so because he was capable. It so happens he was Thomas Cromwell's (from Henry VIII and Thomas More's time) great-great-great-nephew.

2. Bachmann at 225. Parliament later illustrated the power of petitions as political rallying points and symbols when it passed a law during the Restoration of Charles II that neither king nor Parliament would accept a petition from more than ten people.

3. For the history of Lilburne and Cromwell, see **Chapters 5 and 6 of *Bills, Quills, and Stills*, (Constitution Press re-release 2017).**

Van Dyck's 1634 portrait with Charles on a raise making him look taller than his horse

But Cromwell still took the title "His Highness" and signed documents not as "Oliver Cromwell" but "Oliver, P" (for Protector) to emulate King Charles's " R" (for Rex). LOVELL at 350.

AN AGREEMENT OF THE PEOPLE (1647)

Contemporary Satirical print of Cromwell usurping Royal power

See CROMWELL (Columbia Pictures 1970) had Richard Harris in the title role and Alec Guinness as Charles I

John Lilburne

4. "*Congress shall make no law . . . abridging . . . the right of the people peaceably to assemble, and to petition the Government for a redress of grievances.*" U.S. CONST. amend. I.

5. Bachmann at 222.

6. *Quoted in* Bachmann at 208.

7. Again, this history underscores why the First Amendment's Framers coupled the Establishment and Free Exercise Clauses—they learned from history and wanted something better for America.

"*Congress shall make no law respecting an establishment of religion, or prohibiting the free exercise thereof . . .*" U.S. CONST. amend. I.

the one who wanted toleration; Parliament wanted restrictions on both speech and religion. As Charles declared,

"no man shall be disquieted or called in question for differences of opinion in matter of religion which do not disturb the peace of the kingdom."[6]

This was a far cry from his grandfather James I's exclusive support of the established Church of England. But Parliament and society were divided between Anglicans and Puritans, who each wanted to freely *and* intolerantly exercise their faith.[7] With the mix of speech, politics, and religion in mind, the Anglicans got the upper hand in Parliament and codified intolerance with the Clarendon Code.[8] The point was to restrict Puritanism.[9]

Charles tried to soften the law in 1672 by allowing meetings if they secured the crown's preapproval.[10] He also issued two Declarations of Indulgence suspending all penal laws against dissenting Protestants (usually Puritans) and Catholics.

But the Stuarts did not get credit for Charles II's toleration. Part of the reason for this is because he tried to establish a government around an absolute monarch along the French model, which never worked in England.[11] The political reality was that Charles II, just like his father, needed money, and only Parliament could grant it.

---

8. Bachmann at 208–09. The Clarendon Code included:

The **Corporation Act** (1661) providing that only those who received the Anglican communion could be members of the municipal government that controlled elections to Parliament.

The **Act of Uniformity** (1662) expelling two thousand Puritan clergy from their paid positions in the established Anglican Church for not consenting to everything in the PRAYER BOOK.

The **Conventicle Act** (1664) forbidding *"meetings held 'under color or pretence of any exercise of religion' of five or more persons not members of the same household."* This law punished meetings for religious rites other than for the Anglican Church with imprisonment and, for the third offense, transportation to America (and later Australia) upon pain of death for returning to England. Parliament renewed the act in 1670 *"to prevent and suppress seditions conventicles."*

The **Five Mile Act** (1665) forbidding any clergy or school master from coming within five miles of a city or town unless he declared he would not *"at any time endeavor any alteration of Government either in Church or State."* Quoted in Bachmann at 209.

Although the Conventicle Act allowed freedom of worship in the home, the point of the Clarendon Code was to target Independent Puritans, the "dissenters," from the Church of England. These were the folks who loaded up on the *Mayflower* for America.

9. LOVELL at 370–71.

10. Bachmann at 221, *citing* His Majesty's Declaration to All His Loving Subjects (March 15, 1672). Later, Charles's brother James II tried to do the same thing with his 1687 Declaration of Indulgence.

Concurrently, in 1670, a juror named Edward Bushel refused to convict two Quakers who were speaking out in public. One of them was William Penn (later of Pennsylvania). This case ended up being a key to the history of juries and the origin of the Sixth Amendment. See **Chapter 7: Trial by Jury or . . . by God!**

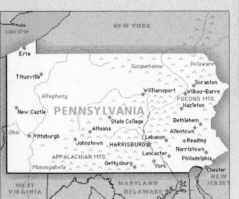

William Penn (1644–1718)

11. LOVELL at 375–77. Charles tried to run the country without Parliament with a "cabal." The political connotation we have for this word comes from the first letters of Charles's five ministers:

Clifford—lord treasurer
Arlington—secretary of state
Buckingham—master of horse
Ashley (Earl of Shaftesbury)—lord chancellor
Lauderdale—secretary for Scottish affairs.

LOVELL at 374. Charles's CABAL was a precursor to a modern cabinet, but its members were not really united to form a government per se. They had their offices because they controlled votes in Parliament.

Flexing its political power, Parliament passed the first Test Act in 1673, requiring all office holders to deny under oath the Catholic doctrine of transubstantiation.[1] This law effectively prevented the king from appointing Catholics to high civil or military posts and disqualified them from serving in Parliament.

Charles II died unexpectedly on February 16, 1685 with no legitimate heir.[2] His brother James II took the throne. James II started out popular but Parliament and the people quickly came to despise him. In addition to the fact that he lacked his brother's tact and ability, he was something even worse: unforgivably Catholic.[3]

In late seventeenth century England, rumors of Catholic plots, conspiracies, and outrages abounded.[4] Beyond rampant prejudice, James II's Catholicism created a constitutional crisis. Since Henry VIII, the king was the head of the Church of England, which James promised Parliament he would defend and support. But how could a Catholic do this?

When James created a new Court of Ecclesiastical Commission to enforce conformity, it was not to Anglicanism, but to Catholicism. This was, to say the least, a bad political move, especially because this court's name was so close to the old Court of High Commission that Parliament had abolished in 1641.[5]

James opened a Catholic chapel in London; surrounded himself with Catholic advisers; and began appointing Catholics to the Privy Council, the faculties of Oxford and Cambridge, and, most disturbing of all, as officers in his rapidly expanding army.[6]

In 1687 and 1688, James issued two Declarations of Indulgence granting free-

---

1. Shown is a **Catholic monstrance** for holding the transubstantiated host. Part of what caused Parliament to pass the Test Acts was the Great Fire of London in 1666, which Londoners blamed on Catholics.

Despite Charles's and later James's attempts to repeal it, the English Test Act remained in effect until The Catholic Relief Act of 1829 (10 Geo. 4, c. 7 (Eng.)). As we will see, the Framers of the U.S. Constitution prohibited "test acts" of any kind at Article VI, section 3: "*no religious Test shall ever be required as a Qualification to any Office or public Trust under the United States.*"

2. On his deathbed in 1685, Charles proclaimed himself a Catholic. Bachmann at 205. The back story is that King Louis of France had been giving Charles a large subsidy under a secret treaty. The deal was that Charles was to declare himself a Catholic and in return he would get French troops to help him. Lovell at 375.

Charles's unexpected death never gave him the chance to carry out the whole plan. But the fact that he went ahead and declared himself a Catholic shows that he at that point must have had some religious feeling—or maybe he was just hedging his bets.

James as lord high admiral

3. Lovell at 389–90 (James II "*was stupid and egocentric*"). James's conversion to Catholicism had come to light with the Test Act. James resigned the office of Lord High Admiral, a post in which he had served honorably and bravely, rather than conform to the Church of England rites.

4. For more discussion of the Titus Oates Popish Plot and the Bloody Assizes see **Chapter 8** et seq. of *Bills, Quills, and Stills*, (**Constitution Press re-release 2017**).

5. Lovell at 390; Bachmann at 214.

6. *See* Bachmann at 205–06, 209; Lovell at 376.

dom of worship to Catholics and Protestant dissidents, abolishing the Test Acts. He also ordered bishops throughout the realm to have the declaration read during church services on two consecutive Sundays.

But instead of earning James credit for toleration, the declarations resulted in seven bishops, including the archbishop of Canterbury, refusing to read the declarations, arguing that the king lacked authority to issue them.[7] James had the bishops arrested for seditious libel.[8]

In our modern way of thinking, what James did was fair and makes him look like a man of principle. After all, why not give Catholics with ability a chance?

The problem was the way he went about it.

James arranged to have a court case to uphold his appointment of Catholic military officers despite the Test Act. He then stacked the deck by making sure the case went before the Court of King's Bench, which he had packed with judges who would give him the ruling he wanted. They held that *"the laws of England are the king's laws,"* and that the king could therefore dispense with the law "*in particular cases and upon particular necessary reasons.*"

Thus, what Protestant England now saw was a Catholic king, creating a Catholic army, with a court that he controlled, saying he was above the law.

Adding to Protestant paranoia was that James's second wife, the very Catholic Mary of Modena, had a baby boy.[9] Thus, unlike his brother Charles II, who kept his Catholicism secret and had the bad fortune (or good sense) not to have a son, James II was starting a Catholic dynasty.

7. Bachmann at 206; *see also* Eric Schnapper, *"Libelou" Petitions for Redress of Grievances: Bad Historiography Makes Worse Law*, 74 IOWA L. REV. 303 (1989) (noting that the First Amendment's Petition Clause owes its origin to the Seven Bishops Case in 1688, which led to the English Bill of Rights of 1689, providing an absolute privilege for the content of petitions to the government); Chemerinsky at 913–15 (noting that in light of the history, the Supreme Court wrongly decided *McDonald v. Smith*, 472 U.S. 479 (1985), which upheld a civil verdict for defamation for the content of letters to President Ronald Reagan and others).

Mary of Modena   Mary's son, James Francis Edward Stuart   Bonnie Prince Charlie

9. Many English regarded Mary of Modena as the Pope's agent. Mary's son was James Francis Edward Stuart, known as The Old Pretender or The Old Chevalier. He was the leader of the first major Jacobite rebellion attempting to regain the throne. "Jacobite" comes from *"Jacobus"* (Latin for "James"). The First Jacobite Rebellion and the Second Jacobite Rebellion were known, respectively, as "The Fifteen" and "The Forty-Five," after the years in which they occurred (i.e., 1715 and 1745). The second significant Jacobite rebellion centered around James II's grandson, Charles Edward Stuart, or Bonnie Prince Charlie. David Niven played him in BONNIE PRINCE CHARLIE (London Film Productions 1948).

    An example of how speech is often symbolic is that those supporting a Stuart restoration would pass a wine glass over a water jug while drinking a toast to "the king" as a clandestine way of toasting the "king over the water," which is to say the Stuart "pretender" in exile in France. *See, e.g.,* WALTER SCOTT, REDGAUNTLET 42 (1824) (describing such a toast but with the words "[o]ver the water" expressly added).

8. Group portrait of the seven bishops imprisoned in the Tower of London in 1688. They were acquitted of charges of seditious libel.

Prominent Englishmen arranged for James's daughter from his first marriage, the comfortably Protestant Mary Stuart, to take over with her comfortably Protestant husband, William of Orange.[1]

Under the banner "the Protestant Religion and the Liberties of England," William landed in England to knock his father-in-law off the throne. In the end, neither James nor his army was up to the fight. Perhaps remembering the execution of his father, Charles I, James fled with his family to France and never returned to England.

Meanwhile, London crowds stormed Catholic churches, and the mayor ordered the disarming of all Catholics. William arrived in London on December 28 and called a "convention."[2] This convention negotiated William and Mary's taking the throne as co-rulers and provided the basis for the English Bill of Rights.

The English Bill of Rights, of course, was the model for our own Bill of Rights. But the English version barred Catholics from the throne of England:

"[I]t hath been found by experience that it is inconsistent with the safety and welfare of this Protestant kingdom to be governed by a papist prince . . . ."[3]

The monarch also had to swear at his coronation he would maintain the Protestant religion.

Thus, we leave the story in Europe and switch to the history the Founders knew in America.

RELIGION AND SPEECH IN PURITAN AMERICA

Puritans and God had a special deal.

God contracted with them,

1. William of Orange

Mary Stuart

2. William technically could not call a Parliament because James II, on his way out of England, burned the writs convening Parliament in December. Parliament could not lawfully be convened unless it was summoned by writs impressed with the Great Seal, but James threw the Great Seal into the Thames River! The convention to work out the outlines of constitutional government set the precedent for America, culminating in the Constitutional Convention of 1789.

3. Through a complicated formula passing though Mary's sister, Princess Anne of Denmark, this would eventually lead to the Hanoverian dynasty in England, which included King George III.

George III

5. Governor John Winthrop of Massachusetts, in his "City on a Hill" sermon, *A Model of Christian Charity*, laid out the deal: "Thus stands the cause between God and us, we are entered into covenant with him for his work; we have taken out a commission . . . . We must be a city on the hill . . . a light to the nations of the world. We must entertain each other in brotherly affection . . . for the supply of other's necessities . . . . We must delight in each other, make other's conditions our own, rejoice together, mourn together, labor and suffer together, always having before our eyes our commission and community in the work, our community as members of the same body . . . . [S]o shall we keep the unity of the spirit in the bond of peace; the Lord will be our God, and delight to dwell among us, as his own people, and will command a blessing upon us in all our ways . . . ." Quoted in Witte, Blest, at 591–92.; also quoted in John Witte, Jr., *How to Govern a City on a Hill: The Early Puritan Contribution to American Constitutionalism*, 39 EMORY L.J. 41, 47 (1990). The "city on a hill" metaphor comes from

4. John Witte, Jr., *Blest Be the Ties That Bind: Covenant and Community in Puritan Thought*, 36 EMORY L.J. 579, 590–91 (1987). According to John Milton, they were "to be agents of His Kingdom, . . . to set a standard [of] truth, . . . to blow the evangelical trumpet to the nations, . . . to give out reformation to the world."

Winthrop

and they contracted with each other, to be the New Jerusalem and chosen people.[4] If they acted "*godly*," God would give them peace and prosperity. It was like the Hebrews' Old Testament deal—take care of God and he will take care of you.[5]

The Puritans, though, expanded the deal, making it not just between God and the chosen people, but between God, the ruler, and the people. This meant that if the people failed, the civil ruler would reprimand them, including the ultimate punishments of banishment or execution.

Conversely, though, the people could compel the ruler to discharge his divine office, and if he failed in his duty toward God or them, they could protest and disobey. And taking a page from the English Civil Wars, they could unseat him "*by force and arms*."[6]

This idea of a special deal with God explains why Puritans both in England and America were so passionate about law and politics.[7] To their way of thinking, a civil ruler had to be godly and the civil law was to reflect divine law and godly order.

Such a covenant implies a theocracy where the state must root out nonconformity and get after the devil.[8] For the Puritans, church and state were technically separate but both under contract with God to achieve the godly end.[9]

At least part of the Puritans' attitude toward government is still with us, notably the idea that the United States is a chosen land and specially blessed people.[10] As a chosen people, we believe in rooting out evil. This has sometimes led to worse evil. But it has also been part this country's drive toward forming a true democratic republic.

Matthew 5:14: "You are the salt of the earth. But if the salt loses its saltiness, how can it be made salty again? It is no longer good for anything, except to be thrown out and trampled by men. You are the light of the world. A city on a hill cannot be hidden. Neither do people light a lamp and put it under a bowl. Instead they put it on its stand, and it gives light to everyone in the house. In the same way, let your light shine before men, that they may see your good deeds and praise your Father in heaven."

6. Witte, *Blest*, at 592–93; Witte, *City on a Hill*, at 59–61. The Puritans insisted that all officials have as "*godly a character*" as possible, notwithstanding their sin. See also Renaud & Weinberger at 80–84 (discussing the nature of church and state government in Puritan America).

9. Witte, *City on a Hill*, at 55.

7. Witte, *Blest*, at 593–94.

8. A sampling includes Anne Hutchinson's heresy trial of 1638, which led to her banishment; Mary Dyer, one of four Quakers known as the Boston martyrs, hanged for repeatedly defying a law banning Quakers; and the notorious Salem witch trials.

10. This approach to religion and society is the jumping off point for many Christian groups such as the Moral Majority, which Jerry Falwell cofounded in 1979 with a "pro-family, pro-life, pro-defense, pro-Israel" agenda. During the 1980s it was one of the largest political lobbies.

After the September 11, 2001, attacks, Falwell said on *The 700 Club*, a daily Christian Conservative TV show: "*I really believe that the pagans, and the abortionists, and the feminists, and the gays and the lesbians who are actively trying to make that an alternative lifestyle, the ACLU, People for the American Way, all of them who have tried to secularize America, I point the finger in their face and say 'you helped this happen.'*" Falwell further stated that the attacks were "*probably deserved.*" After heavy criticism, Falwell apologized, though he later stood by his statement, declaring "*if we decide to change all the rules on which this Judeo-Christian nation was built, we cannot expect the Lord to put his shield of protection around us as he has in the past.*"

By the late 1980s the Moral Majority dissolved, and Falwell died in 2007. The Christian Coalition of America continues much the same political agenda. Regarding early nineteenth century religious fundamentalism of the Second Great Awakening, John Adams warned that "*instead of the most enlightened people, I fear we Americans shall soon have the character of the silliest people under Heaven.*" Stone at 14, *quoting* Letter from John Adams to Benjamin Rush (Dec. 28, 1807).

John Adams

The Puritans did wish to create a Christian community.[1] But the Founding Fathers were generations removed from Puritan zeal. As we will see, the Framers of the Constitution and Bill of Rights were reacting to their own forefathers to create a secular state.

PRESSING RELIGION IN ENGLAND AND AMERICA

The Puritans were keen on getting their message out; the printing press was how they did it. By 1638, the Massachusetts Bay Colony had its own printing press.[2]

With the Puritans' "city on a hill" mentality, the division between church and state was only technical.

If you disagreed with one, you disagreed with the other. A statement about religion was political, and a political statement was religious.

Thus licensing continued in the American colonies long after it ended in England in 1695.[3] With government and religion mixed, controlling the press became very important. All the colonies outlawed or censored *"blasphemous"*

---

1. Islands of Tolerance in an Intolerant World: Rhode Island and Pennsylvania. Albert at 39–40. Pennsylvania and Rhode Island had no established church: *"Pennsylvania, because its founding Quakers believed in it, and Rhode Island, because Roger Williams thought everyone but him so reprobate that they might as well worship as they pleased."* RICHARD BROOKHISER, WHAT WOULD THE FOUNDERS DO? 26–27 (2006); see also J. WILLIAM FROST, A PERFECT FREEDOM: RELIGIOUS LIBERTY IN PENNSYLVANIA 18 (1990) (*"In Pennsylvania, there would be no legal church establishment, no tithes or forced maintenance of any minister."*). Pennsylvania was not quite as open as Rhode Island because its religious freedom only applied to those *"who acknowledge[d] the being of a God"* and, like other states, had a religious requirement for holding public office. Nevertheless, it was a place where a man with freethinking ideas like Benjamin Franklin could live, prosper, and thrive.

Benjamin Franklin

Roger Williams

Colonial Pennsylvania

Colonial Rhode Island

2. Robert A. Rutland, *Freedom of the Press*, in THE BILL OF RIGHTS: A LIVELY HERITAGE 32 (John Kukla ed., 1987). Indeed, the press came before the colony's first legal code, The Massachusetts Body of Liberties of 1641.

3. Regarding licensing in England and the relative freedom of the press, see LOVELL at 399.

---

4. Milton's liberal thoughts on free speech did not extend to blasphemy, treason, or defamation, and they must be subject to *"the sharpest justice"* against the *"malefactors."* But not even this bad speech justified a prior restraint for Milton. To censor a book is to deny human nature. Witte, *Milton*, at 1594–95.

Of course, many would consider *"Bong Hits 4 Jesus"* blasphemy. Blasphemy is clearly subject to interpretation.

Is Morgan Freeman or George Burns playing God blasphemy in BRUCE ALMIGHTY (Universal Studios 2003), EVAN ALMIGHTY (Universal Studios 2007) and OH, GOD (Warner Bros. 1977)? What about other depictions of religious symbols for humor or dramatic impact? And what about artistic expression in a free society?

Image by Helen Koop

speech, such as denying the soul's immortality or the Holy Trinity.[4] Generally, the laws that outlawed blasphemy also prohibited speaking badly of ministers and royalty.[5]

If blasphemy is putting a religious truth in a negative light, then *libel*, the putting of a person or entity in a negative light, is closely related.

LIBEL LAW IN ENGLAND AND COLONIAL AMERICA

Libel is a kind of *defamation*, which is when someone publishes (i.e., makes public) a statement that makes someone else look bad.[6] If you couple the libel with a statement against the government it becomes *seditious libel*, i.e., encouraging sedition.

The concept of seditious libel was always accordion-like, dependent on the whim of kings and their judges.[7] William Blackstone in 1769 clarified that English law allowed no prior restraint or censorship:

"Every freeman has an undoubted right to lay what sentiments he pleases before the public, but if he publishes what is improper, mischievous, or illegal, he must take the consequences of his own temerity."[8]

Piss Christ was Andres Serrano's 1987 artistic photo of a small plastic crucifix submerged in a glass of his urine. The piece won the Southeastern Center for Contemporary Art's "Awards in the Visual Arts" competition, which the National Endowment for the Arts (NEA), a United States government agency, sponsored. Religious groups such as the American Family Association and legislators objected, and the NEA nearly lost government funding.

NATIONAL
ENDOWMENT
FOR THE ARTS
A great nation
deserves great art.

5. Regarding speaking in a religious assembly against the government and its prohibition, see LEVY, ORIGINS OF THE BILL OF RIGHTS 113–14 (1999).

6. If the offending material is "published" as spoken words or sounds, sign language, gestures, etc., it is *slander*. But if it is published in writing, film, CD, or DVD, it is *libel*. *Calumny* and *vilification* are synonyms for defamation. In the Bible, *Proverbs* 10:18 states: "*He that uttereth a slander, is a fool.*"
  See J.W. EHRLICH, THE HOLY BIBLE AND THE LAW 155 (1962).

7. Seditious libel was malicious, scandalous political falsehoods that tended to breach the peace, instill revulsion or contempt in the people against their government, or lower their esteem for their rulers. LEVY, BILL OF RIGHTS, at 122.
  One of the key sources on this history, if not the key source, is LEONARD W. LEVY, EMERGENCE OF A FREE PRESS (1985). Several commentators, however, take exception to Levy's earlier work, LEONARD W. LEVY, LEGACY OF SUPPRESSION (1960), including David A. Anderson, *Levy vs. Levy*, 84 MICH. L. REV. 777 (1986) (reviewing *Emergence of a Free Press*). Levy has responded in various articles, including Leonard W. Levy, *On the Origins of the Free Press Clause*, 32 UCLA L. REV. 177 (1984) and Leonard W. Levy, *The Legacy Reexamined*, 37 STAN. L. REV. 767 (1985). *See* David M. Rabban, *The Ahistorical Historian: Leonard Levy on Freedom of Expression in Early American History*, 37 STAN. L. REV. 795 (1985) (book review).
  Also taking on Levy is LARRY D. ELDRIDGE, A DISTANT HERITAGE: THE GROWTH OF FREE SPEECH IN EARLY AMERICA 3 (1994) (arguing "*that colonists experienced a dramatic expansion of their freedom to criticize government and its officials across the seventeenth century*").

8. *Quoted in* O'Brien at 44. Blackstone's *Commentaries* was *the* book every colonial lawyer used for both his training and practice.

William Blackstone

Thus, the law allowed for later prosecution of "bad" speech:

> "[W]here blasphemous, immoral, treasonable, schismatical, seditious, or scandalous libels are punished by the English law . . . the liberty of the press, properly understood, is by no means infringed or violated."[1]

And, for such "bad" speech, the defendant "*shall on a fair and impartial trial be adjudged of a pernicious tendency . . . .*"

This, for Blackstone,

> "*is necessary for the preservation of peace and good order, of government and religion, the only solid foundations of civil liberty.*"[2]

Eighteenth century England, however, saw few prosecutions for seditious libel because the press was part of one political faction or another and "*even the most scummy had powerful political backers.*"[3]

Thus, even though no written constitution protected it, the eighteenth century English press in practice was relatively free. In fact, it was ahead of the American press in its freedom to criticize as it pleased.

Perhaps owing to its longer tradition of control over the press for religious reasons,

---

1. William Blackstone, Commentaries *151–52 (1769), reprinted in L. Levy, Freedom of the Press from Zenger to Jefferson 104–05 (1966). Many of the founding generation agreed with Blackstone. See Levy, *Free Press Clause*, at 205, noting that in 1788 Jefferson urged Madison to add a bill of rights to the Constitution, stating that "[a] declaration that the federal government will never restrain the presses from printing anything they please, will not take away the liability of the printers for false facts printed." Letter from Thomas Jefferson to James Madison (July 31, 1788). One of Jefferson's political rivals, Alexander Hamilton, in 1804 defended a Federalist editor prosecuted by the New York attorney general for libeling President Jefferson, saying that "*the liberty of the press . . . [is] publishing the truth, for good motives and for justifiable ends . . . .*" But an editor could not "*use the weapon of truth wantonly . . . for relating that which does not appertain to official conduct [or for] disturbing the peace of families.*" According to Hamilton, this was not "*fair and honest exposure*" and was thus libelous. Quoted in Brookhiser at 161.

2. Blackstone's fuller quote follows: *[W]here blasphemous, immoral, treasonable, schismatical, seditious, or scandalous libels are punished by the English law . . . the liberty of the press, properly understood, is by no means infringed or violated . . . The liberty of the press is indeed essential to the nature of a free state; but this consists in laying no previous restraints upon publications, and not in freedom from censure for criminal matter when published. Every freeman has an undoubted right to lay what sentiments he pleases before the public; to forbid this is to destroy the freedom of the press; but if he publishes what is improper, mischievous, or illegal, he must take the consequences of his own temerity. . . . But to punish (as the law does at present) any dangerous or offensive writings, which, when published, shall on a fair and impartial trial be adjudged of a pernicious tendency, is necessary for the preservation of peace and good order, of government and religion, the only solid foundations of civil liberty. Thus the will of individuals is still left free; the abuse only of that free will is the object of legal punishment. Neither is any restraint hereby laid upon freedom of thought or inquiry: liberty of private sentiment is still left; the disseminating or making public of bad sentiments, destructive of the ends of society, is the crime which society corrects.* Quoted in Levy, Freedom of the Press, at 104–05.

3. Levy, *Free Press Clause,* at 183–84.

4. In 1722, for example, a young Benjamin Franklin and his brother James, publisher of Boston's *New England Courant*, were brought before the Massachusetts Assembly to reveal the authors of several "libelous" articles. They refused, and the Assembly censured and jailed James for one month but let Benjamin off with a warning. Scott J. Street, *Poor Richard's Forgotten Press Clause: How Journalists Can Use Original Intent to Protect Their Confidential Sources*, 27 Loy. L.A. Ent. L. Rev. 463, 465 (2007).

Benjamin later attacked censorship in Poor Richard's Almanack (1757): "*This Nurse of Arts, and Freedom's Fence, To chain, is Treason against Sense: And Liberty, thy thousand Tongues None silence who design no Wrongs; For those that use the Gag's Restraint, First rob, before they stop Complaint.*" Quoted in Street at 463.

Franklin also supported the written word by helping start the first public library in America—and inventing bifocals! Brookhiser at 19.

1739 edition of Poor Richard's Almanac

5. Levy, Bill of Rights, at 108.

or because America consisted of colonies under England's control, the colonial press did not enjoy the same freedom.[4] Through the 1760s colonial governments held publishers criminally liable if they abused the right to speech.[5]

The test of whether an accused in a libel case could have a *"fair and impartial"* trial happened in America.[6] In analyzing libel law, Blackstone left open two fundamental questions:

- Is truth a defense, and

- Does the jury or judge decide if there was a malicious libel?

A court case called *Zenger* would decide both questions for America.

THE ZENGER TRIAL

John Peter Zenger's 1735 trial revolutionized the law of seditious libel.

Zenger's *New York Weekly Journal* printed essays as well as advertisements and letters about local issues (generally printed under pseudonyms).[7] Its specialty, though, was attacking New York's royal governor, William Cosby. Sometimes Zenger would print a letter and leave a few dashes followed by,

"Something is here omitted, for which I beg my correspondent to excuse, as not safe for me to print."[8]

6. The Small Penis Rule: Modern American libel cases often involve an author making a fictional portrait of a real person, and that person suing. The "small penis rule" is an informal strategy that allows an author to evade a libel suit. A 1998 *New York Times* article describes the rule as follows:

> "'For a fictional portrait to be actionable, it must be so accurate that a reader of the book would have no problem linking the two,' said Mr. Friedman. Thus, he continued, libel lawyers have what is known as 'the small penis rule.' One way authors can protect themselves from libel suits is to say that a character has a small penis. 'Now no male is going to come forward and say, 'That character with a very small penis, that's me!'"

Dinitia Smith, "Writers as Plunderers; Why Do They Keep Giving Away Other People's Secrets? N.Y. TIMES, Oct. 24, 1998, *available at* http://www.nytimes.com/1998/10/24/books/writers-as-plunderers-why-do-they-keep-giving-away-other-people-s-secrets. html?sec=&spon=&pagewanted=2.

7. Street at 462–66, noting the Founders' familiarity with Zenger's case.

Sir William Cosby

8. JAMES ALEXANDER, A BRIEF NARRATIVE OF THE CASE AND TRIAL OF JOHN PETER ZENGER, PRINTER OF THE NEW YORK WEEKLY JOURNAL 9 (1963).

The slogan of the *New York Times* is *"all the news that's fit to print"* not *"all the news that's safe to print."* The Pentagon Papers put the slogan to the test. THE PENTAGON PAPERS (officially titled UNITED STATES–VIETNAM RELATIONS, 1945–1967: A STUDY PREPARED BY THE DEPARTMENT OF DEFENSE) was a top secret U.S. Defense Department history of U.S. involvement in Vietnam from 1945 to 1967. Defense Secretary Robert S. McNamara commissioned the study in 1967–68. They revealed that the United States had deliberately expanded the war by carpet bombing Cambodia and Laos, raiding North Vietnam's coast, and expanding Marine Corps attacks, all previously unreported.

After Daniel Ellsberg leaked *The Pentagon Papers* to the *New York Times*, President Richard Nixon got a federal court to stop publication. The Supreme Court quickly heard the case and rejected the government's argument. *New York*

Robert McNamara   Daniel Ellsberg

Times Co. v. United States, 403 U.S. 713 (1971). In a concurring opinion, Justice Hugo L. Black wrote: *In the First Amendment the Founding Fathers gave the free press the protection it must have to fulfill its essential role in our democracy . . . . The press was protected so that it could bare the secrets of government and inform the people. Only a free and unrestrained press can effectively expose deception in government. And paramount among the responsibilities of a free press is the duty to prevent any part of the government from deceiving the people and sending them off to distant lands to die of foreign fevers and foreign shot and shell.*

For Ellsberg and the events leading to the Pentagon Paper's publication, see the very good documentary, THE MOST DANGEROUS MAN IN AMERICA: DANIEL ELLSBERG and THE PENTAGON PAPERS (First Run Features 2009)

The speculation from this statement probably caused more impact than if Zenger had actually printed it. Zenger also would often use made-up ads,[1] one of which described Cosby as a monkey.

Zenger celebrated the September 1734 city elections of antiroyalist magistrates with an anonymous article calling Cosby and his supporters "*pettyfogging knaves*" and asserting that the new magistrates would "*make the scoundrel rascals fly.*"[2] Zenger refused to divulge the author.

Zenger was obviously looking for trouble, and governor Cosby gave it to him.

Cosby tried to have a grand jury indict Zenger, but three different colonial grand juries refused. Cosby eventually had to convince the New York Council to arrest Zenger, and it also issued a warrant to burn four issues of the *Weekly Journal*.

For his 1735 seditious libel trial, Zenger could not find a New York lawyer to help him. The governor had disqualified some, and the rest thought his case a loser. Finally, a Philadelphia lawyer named Andrew Hamilton (no relation to Alexander Hamiton) took his case.[3]

Hamilton vigorously defended Zenger and an individual's freedom to criticize the government:

1. Over 250 years after *Zenger*, *Hustler Magazine* publisher Larry Flynt was still using made-up ads ridiculing opponents. In *Hustler Magazine, Inc. v. Falwell*, 485 U.S. 46 (1988), the Supreme Court dealt with Flynt's made-up ad featuring a "Jerry Falwell" interview about having sex with his mother.

In small print the "ad" disclaimed "*ad parody—not to be taken seriously.*"

Falwell was not amused. He sued Flynt for libel, invasion of privacy, and intentional infliction of emotional distress. The trial court dismissed the invasion of privacy claim and the jury found in favor of Flynt on the libel claim but for Falwell on intentional infliction of emotional distress, awarding Falwell $150,000 in damages.

The Supreme Court eventually heard the case and unanimously ruled that the First Amendment prohibits awarding damages to public figures for emotional distress. Any other ruling would "*chill*" valid political speech. "*The appeal of the political cartoon or caricature is often based on exploitation of unfortunate physical traits or politically embarrassing events— an exploitation often calculated to injure the feelings of the subject of the portrayal.*" Thus, even though Falwell argued that the *Hustler* ad was too "*outrageous*" for First Amendment protection, "outrageous" is a subjective term, and such a standard "*runs afoul of our longstanding refusal to allow damages to be awarded because the speech in question may have an adverse emotional impact on the audience.*"

THE PEOPLE V. LARRY FLYNT (Columbia Pictures 1996) depicts Flynt's story and his legal clashes, including the *Falwell* case. Flynt had a cameo as the trial judge.

Flynt and Falwell after the Supreme Court arguments, and Flynt and Falwell appearing together on *Larry King Live* on January 10, 1997. Both apparently got a lot out of the controversy.

Image by Helen Koop

"I beg leave to insist that the right of complaining or remonstrating is natural; and the restraint upon this natural right is the law only, and those restraints can only extend to what is false."[4]

Hamilton was advancing a new idea in libel cases that government regulation could only restrain what was false. Rather than focusing only on whether the publisher *"maliciously"* put the government in a negative light, whether true or not, truth was a defense. And the jury decided the truth.[5] What this meant is that a jury could nullify any government prosecution of a publisher or writer.

With this approach, Hamilton challenged the law itself, not just the facts. The jury bought it; the one-day trial ended with the jury deliberating for a few minutes and acquitting Zenger.[6]

Zenger's trial expanded the idea of press freedom, and this idea shaped colonial journalism leading to the Revolution.[7] And incorporating this concept is the First Amendment:

"Congress shall make no law . . . abridging the freedom of speech, or of the press . . . ."

Zenger's trial created an environment that allowed a freer press than ever before.[8]

---

2. ALEXANDER at 13–14, 111.

3. Hamilton, ironically, had participated in Pennsylvania's prosecution of publisher Andrew Bradford for seditious libel in 1729. ALEXANDER at 22. *See also* R. BLAIN ANDRUS, LAWYER: A BRIEF 5,000 YEAR HISTORY 109–10 (2009).

Andrew Hamilton

5. LEVY, BILL OF RIGHTS, at 104–05, 114.

Hamilton 1904 watch

6. Hamilton was already one of the greatest lawyers of his day. After Zenger's trial the term "Philadelphia lawyer" became synonymous with smart lawyer.

Andrew's son, James Hamilton, also became a prominent lawyer and Pennsylvanian politician. He died in 1793, but had owned a large track of land in Lancaster, Pennsylvania, where investors later established the Hamilton Watch Company—named after him—in 1892.

7. For a brief discussion of the Zenger case in the context of the growth of the American jury system, see Albert W. Alschuler & Andrew G. Deiss, *A Brief History of the Criminal Jury in the United States,* 61 U. CHI. L. REV. 867, 871–74 (1994). Clarence Darrow cited the William Penn and John Peter Zenger trials and juries in the closing argument of his own trial. *See* GEOFFREY COWAN, THE PEOPLE V. CLARENCE DARROW: THE BRIBERY TRIAL OF AMERICA'S GREATEST LAWYER (1993). *See also* **Chapter 7: Trial by Jury or . . . by God!**

8. *See McIntyre v. Ohio Elections Comm'n,* 514 U.S. 334, 361 (1995) (Thomas, J., concurring) (noting the Zenger trial's significance).

Only later in England did the Fox Libel Act of 1792 allow the jury to return a simple verdict of not guilty in libel cases. LOVELL at 457.

Hamilton's closing argument

4. ALEXANDER at 84.

REPUBLICAN JOURNALISM

People who bemoan the state of modern American journalism and politics should compare it to that of colonial America through the early republic.[1]

Today most media outlets maintain at least the semblance of objectivity, trying to present both sides of an issue.

Back then, most of the reporting looked like op-eds.[2] Many newspapers, in fact, were not independent but aligned with one party or the other.[3]

Journalists, in fact, were often proxies for the politicians or parties.[4]

But because journalists were not "gentlemen," they did not bother dueling each other or their targets, unlike the politicians for whom they worked.[5]

During the colonial period after the *Zenger* case, the crown could not use the criminal law to control libel.[6] Thus the greatest American journalist of the

1. Critics point to the *Howard Stern Show* as but one example of modern journalism gone amok. But, though more sexual, Stern would have fit right into early America. *See* Levy, *Reexamined*, at 768 ("*For the most part, people understood that scummy journalism unavoidably accompanied the benefits to be gained from a free press.*"); *see also* Levy, *Free Press Clause*, at 218 ("*Anyone who has read American newspapers from 1776 to 1791, when the first press clauses in the state constitutions and the first amendment were framed, would realize that the American press, like the British, was astonishingly scurrilous.*").

2. Partisan politics increased the number of newspapers in the United States from 92 in 1790 to 329 at the end of Thomas Jefferson's presidency, with all but 56 identified with a political party. *See Thomas Jefferson: Establishing a Federal Republic,* LIBRARY OF CONGRESS, http://www.loc.gov/exhibits/jefferson/jefffed.html (last visited Nov. 20, 2009).

3. *See,* for example, the *National Gazette,* the Jeffersonian Republicans' first newspaper (Nov. 14, 1791). Jefferson and Madison financially supported it and gave its editor, Philip Freneau, a position in Jefferson's State Department.

4. "Infant Liberty Nursed by Mother Mob." The Federalists hoped to regain the presidency with this anti-Jefferson political cartoon. It failed with James Madison's election in 1809.

Jefferson got it turned back on him with "The Providential Detection" (1797–1800), showing Jefferson kneeling before

the altar of Gallic despotism as God and an American eagle save the Constitution. Jefferson's alleged attack on George Washington and John Adams in a letter to Philip Mazzei falls from his other hand. Satan, the writings of Thomas Paine, and French philosophers support Jefferson.

5. BROOKHISER at 142–45. Partly to maintain their stature as gentlemen, the Founders all used pseudonyms for their writing and reporting. Even James Madison, Alexander Hamilton, and John Jay wrote THE FEDERALIST PAPERS under the pseudonym "Publius".

In one famous case it did not work. Hamilton and Burr sparred in the papers for years, each doing the best he could to destroy the other's reputation. Finally, their cold war went hot, and Burr mortally wounded Hamilton in a duel on July 11, 1804, ending both their careers.

Brur-Hamilton duel

age, Benjamin Franklin, had all the freedom he needed to both become a rich man and a leader of the Revolution.[7] This, combined with his job as deputy postmaster for the colonies, put Franklin in position to influence events.[8]

Like good journalists today, Franklin the journalist protected his sources—and it cost him.

In 1773, a Franklin paper, *The Boston Gazette*, published private letters of Massachusetts royal Governor Thomas Hutchinson and Lieutenant Governor Andrew Oliver. In the letters, Hutchinson encouraged London to crack down on his fellow Bostonians, writing "[t]here must be an

abridgement of what are called English liberties."[9]

Back in London, where Franklin had been living for nine years, recriminations flew as to who leaked the letters. Two "gentlemen" fools even fought a duel while protesting their innocence. Because of this, Franklin admitted he leaked the letters.[10]

A colonial press   John Wilkes

6. Levy, *Free Press Clause,* at 218. Just before the Revolution, America was abuzz about Englishman John Wilkes and his case, *Wilkes v. Wood.* Rutland at 33. In 1763 Wilkes, a prominent Parliament member, published anonymous pamphlets called *The North Briton,* including No. 45, which sharply criticized King George III. Government officials searched Wilkes's home, seized his papers, and arrested him. Such general warrants were common at the time to muzzle the press and squelch political dissent. Wilkes sued and won! *See* **Chapter 4: Molasses and the Sticky Origins of the Fourth Amendment,** which extensively discusses Wilkes as a precursor of the Fourth Amendment. *See* Daniel J. Solove, *The First Amendment as Criminal Procedure,* 82 N.Y.U. L. REV. 112 (2007) (noting that the First, Fourth, and Fifth Amendments share a common background concerning seditious libel). *See also* Levy, *Free Press Clause,* at 216 (noting that Wilkes held orthodox opinions regarding the common law of seditious libel).

8. Franklin's political cartoon "Join, or Die" urged the colonies to join together during the French and Indian War. This is the first political cartoon in an American newspaper. STEPHEN HESS & SANDY NORTHROP, DRAWN & QUARTERED: THE HISTORY OF AMERICAN POLITICAL CARTOONS 24 (1996).

JOIN, or DIE.

9. BROOKHISER at 139; *see also* Street at 463.

7. Regarding Franklin, the press and mail, and the advanced state of journalism in the colonies, *see* BROOKHISER at 19–20 (reporting that there were twenty-five newspapers in the thirteen colonies, many set up by Franklin or his apprentices).

One of Franklin's newspapers was the *Pennsylvania Gazette*

The word "gazette" for newspaper came from sixteenth century Venice, where Venetians would use a "*gazeta,*" a small coin, to buy their newspapers, a "*gazeta de la novita,*" literally "a pennyworth of news." AYTO at 251; ROBERT HENDRICKSON, QPB ENCYCLOPEDIA OF WORD AND PHRASE ORIGINS 289 (2004).

Thomas Hutchinson   Andrew Oliver

10. Franklin's protestations that he only released the letters to a few local leaders to show that their problems were just with an overzealous Hutchinson ring disingenuous. BROOKHISER at 140. Franklin was sixty-eight years old, having made his first fame and fortune as a journalist. He knew better than anyone the way of the press.

But he would not reveal his "Deep Throat."[1]

In January 1774, a committee of the Privy Council called him in for interrogation; Franklin wouldn't budge.[2] Just like Zenger in 1735, Franklin stood on the principle that a journalist should not reveal his sources.[3] He took it to his grave.[4]

Confidentiality of sources became a principle of American journalism.[5] But because Franklin would not reveal the source of the Hutchinson letters, he lost his lucrative job as deputy postmaster general for all North America and could no longer serve as lobbyist for four American colonies.[6]

Franklin left London in March 1775, never to return as a British subject.

1. "Deep Throat" refers to the main whistleblower in the Watergate scandal. The name came from the 1972 pornographic movie DEEP THROAT (Plymouth Distribution and Bryanston Distritbution 1972) and is now synonymous for confidential whistleblower.

Washington Post reporters Bob Woodward and Carl Bernstein broke and followed the story of the burglary of the Democratic headquarters at the Watergate complex. The trail led to the downfall of President Richard Nixon in 1972. Dustin Hoffman and Robert Redford played Woodward and Bernstein in ALL THE PRESIDENT'S MEN (Warner Brothers 1976).

Nixon leaving office

The Watergate complex

Nixon announces Resignation

Resignation Letter

2. Even after an hour of abuse from Solicitor General Alexander Wedderburn who harangued, "*I hope, my lords, you will mark and brand this man [Franklin], for the honour of this country, of Europe, and of mankind .. ... Men will watch him with a jealous eye; they will hide their papers from him and lock up their escritoires. He will henceforth esteem it a libel to be called a man of letters.*" Quoted in BROOKHISER at 140–41. This interrogation finally turned Franklin into a revolutionary.

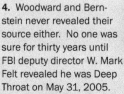
Wedderburn

Franklin in 1777

3. Regarding the importance of *Zenger* as precedent of keeping a reporter's sources confidential, *see McIntyre v. Ohio Elections Comm'n*, 514 U.S. 334, 361 (1995) (Thomas, J., concurring) (Zenger's trial "*signified at an early moment the extent to which anonymity and the freedom of the press were intertwined in the early American mind*").

4. Woodward and Bernstein never revealed their source either. No one was sure for thirty years until FBI deputy director W. Mark Felt revealed he was Deep Throat on May 31, 2005.

5. The Big Fat Freedom of the Press. In 1958 journalist Marie Torre quoted a CBS network executive that "*something is bothering [Judy Garland] .. . I don't know, but I wouldn't be surprised if it's because she thinks she's terribly fat.*" Garland sued CBS and her lawyers eventually deposed Torre, who refused to identify her source because if she did "*nobody in the business [would] talk to [her] again.*" *Garland v. Torre*, 259 F.2d 545, 547–48 (2d Cir. 1958). The court put Torre in jail for ten days for contempt of court for refusing to divulge her source. The courts of various states remain split on whether reporters can refuse to name their sources. *See, e.g., State v. Knops*, 183 N.W.2d 93, 95 (Wis. 1971) (constitutional privilege exists but subject to public's overriding need to know in the interests of justice); *State v. Buchanan*, 436 P.2d 729, 732 (Or. 1968) (reporters have no constitutional right to protect sources though it could be created by statute). *See generally* Street at 469.

Garland in the *Wizard of Oz* (1939) — Garland putting on makeup in 1957 — Marie Torre

When the British eventually implemented Governor Hutchinson's advice and "abridged" "what are called English liberties," the colonies predictably reacted. The Stamp Act of 1764, for instance, would have put a modest tax on colonial newspapers, but in defiance not a single newspaper appeared on stamped paper.[7]

As for the press and journalism during the Revolution, there was a double standard. Patriot newspapers were free but not the pro-British loyalist ones.[8] This set a precedent that has carried through American history: freedom of speech and press suffer during war.[9] If we accept, as the Framers did, the vital role free speech plays in a healthy democracy, then hindering speech even during war is a contradiction and betrayal.

6. But Franklin ended up on the first U.S. postage stamp in 1847. And, he later made it onto the $100 bill, perhaps for his quote from POOR RICHARD'S ALMANAC: "A penny saved is twopence dear" (misquoted as "A penny saved is a penny earned").

7. Rutland at 33.

8. Rutland at 34. *See also* Levy, *Re-examined,* at 767 (noting "*that tarring and feathering a Tory editor because of his opinions shows a rather restricted meaning and scope of the freedom of the press. Indeed, one may ask whether there was free speech during the Revolutionary era if only the speech of freedom was free.*").

9. *See generally* GEOFFREY R. STONE'S PERILOUS TIMES: FREE SPEECH IN WARTIME, *From* THE SEDITION ACT OF 1798 *to the* WAR ON TERRORISM (2004) for a historical survey of freedom of speech during America's wars and an eloquent defense of free speech. "*[T]he national government has never attempted to punish opposition to government policies, except in time of war.*"

- Shortly after the Revolution, President John Adams and the Federalists enacted the Sedition Act of 1798 prohibiting any person from writing, publishing or uttering anything of a "*false, scandalous and malicious*" nature against the government. Though supposedly because of an impending war with France, the act served primarily as a political weapon to strengthen the Federalists.
- During the Civil War, President Abraham Lincoln suspended the writ of habeas corpus eight times for persons who had been arrested for speaking or

writing against his administration. A president can suspend habeas corpus during war, but Lincoln would refer to the Civil War as a "war"—rather than an insurrection—only when it suited him. *See* Rutland at 38,

Lincoln as a Phoenix raising himself by burning free speech and habeas corpus

noting that during the Civil War the Confederacy allowed more free press than in the Union, where federal marshals and mobs intimidated the war's Northern critics.

- During World War I, the government prosecuted around two thousand people for opposing the war and the draft under the Espionage Act of 1917 and Sedition Act of 1918. These people generally received ten- to twenty-year sentences. President Woodrow Wilson, while arguing to "*make the world safe for democracy,*" unsuccessfully pushed for a censorship law, arguing that "*authority to exercise censorship over the press*" was "*absolutely necessary to the public safety.*" *See* O'Brien at 47, noting that by the end of World War I, thirty-two states had laws against criminal syndication or sedition.
- Just before World War II, a congressional committee began investigating "*the extent, character and objects of un-American propaganda activities in the United States*"; the FBI established an aggressive informer program and Congress passed the Alien Registration Act of 1940 (the Smith Act), which forbade individuals to advocate the propriety of overthrowing the government by force. Ironically,

much of these provisions had to do with a perceived fight against communism, but the Soviet Union ended up our ally in World War II. Much of World War II propaganda was to try to get people to talk less with "*loose lips sink ships*" as the slogan.

- During the Cold War, President Harry Truman established a loyalty program for all civilian government employees; the House Un-American Activities Committee, or HUAC, cited 135 people for contempt (more than the entire Congress had cited for contempt in the history of the country to that point); and Senator Joseph R. McCarthy launched his virulent rampage.
- During the Vietnam War, the FBI carried out a wide-ranging program to "*expose, disrupt and otherwise neutralize*" dissident political activities, and protesters were prosecuted for burning their draft cards and expressing contempt for the American flag.

One of the Alien and Sedition Acts

But so far, America has always bounced back from these wartime restrictions with expanded liberty.[1] This expansion conforms to James Madison's original vision of an expansive freedom of speech and press,[2] often despite the wishes of our government.[3]

If the press of Madison's day is any indication, blatantly partisan, rasping, corrosive, and offensive discussions on all topics of public interest were the norm.[4] In fact, it makes much of what passes for

J. Edgar Hoover was the director of the FBI, from March 22, 1935 to May 2, 1972

1. Again, see generally STONE noting that *"the major restrictions of civil liberties of the past would be less thinkable today than they were in 1798, 1861, 1917, 1942, 1950 or 1969,"* and that *"in terms of both the evolution of constitutional doctrine and the development of a national culture more attuned to civil liberties, the United States has made substantial progress."* Stone notes, among other examples of progress, *New York Times Co. v. United States (Pentagon Papers),* 403 U.S. 713 (1971), where *"the Supreme Court, for the first time in American history, stood tall—in wartime—for the First Amendment."*

As Stone argues, *"we may learn slowly, and only in fits and starts, but we do learn."* For example, a congressional report declared that the Sedition Act of 1798 had been passed under a *"mistaken exercise"* of power and was *"null and void."* The Sedition Act of 1918, which was repealed two years later, helped give birth to the modern civil liberties movement. In 1976, President Gerald Ford formally prohibited the CIA from using electronic or physical surveillance to collect information on domestic activities of Americans and FBI Director Clarence Kelly publicly apologized for abuses under J. Edgar Hoover.

2. Alien and Sedition Acts. In 1789 the Federalist Congress passed and President John Adams signed An Act for the Punishment of Certain Crimes against the United States, four laws making it a crime to publish *"false, scandalous, and malicious writing"* against the government or its officials. The point was to punish criticism of Adams. Of course, gagging the Republican press and criticism of Adam's onetime friend and then political rival Vice President Thomas Jefferson was fair game! LEVY, BILL OF RIGHTS, at 125–26; Rutland at 38.

A court fined Vermont Congressman Matthew Lyon $1,000 and sentenced him to four months in an unheated cell in winter for suggesting that Adams be sent to a madhouse. BROOKHISER at 44. When Jefferson took over as president in 1801, he pardoned all the journalists convicted under the act, which expired on March 3, 1801. Rutland at 38. Lyon has the distinction of being the only man elected to Congress from jail—and the first to have an ethics charge against him for spitting on Roger Griswold.

But, something not generally understood is that the Sedition Act embodied Zengerian reforms in that it allowed the defendant to plead truth as a defense and confirmed that a jury would decide guilt, exactly what eighteenth century libertarians had fought for. Levy, *Free Press Clause,* at 199–200. Supreme Court Justice William J. Brennan, Jr. cited the Sedition Act in *New York Times v. Sullivan,* 376 U.S. 254, 273, 276 (1964), because it *"first crystallized a national awareness of the central meaning of the First Amendment"* and although *"never tested in this Court, the attack upon its validity has carried the day in the court of history."*

Contemporary cartoon of fight in Congress over the Alien and Sedition Acts between Matthew Lyon (with tongs) and Roger Griswold of Connecticut

Jefferson in 1791

3. Levy, *Reexamined,* at 769. Jefferson's draft of the 1783 constitution for Virginia proposed that the press *"shall be subject to no other restraint than liableness to legal prosecution for false facts printed and published."* LEVY, BILL OF RIGHTS, at 109.

But when Jefferson became president, he happily persecuted Federalist newspapermen. In 1806, his administration prosecuted six Connecticut citizens for seditious libel against him. Two of the defendants committed the crime while preaching sermons and the others in newspaper. Levy, *Free Press Clause,* at 177. Jefferson also had Harry Croswell, an obscure Federalist editor, prosecuted for seditious libel. LEVY, BILL OF RIGHTS, at 131.

Jefferson in 1800

Thus Jefferson, once in power, asserted that the rival press could criminally assault the government, giving the government legal recourse. *Id.* at 109.

4. The ancient Athenian Demosthenes explained that *"of all states,"* democracies are *"the most antagonistic"* to political leaders *"of infamous habits"* because *"every man is at liberty to publish their shame."* Indeed, *"even the lone individual, uttering the deserved reproach, makes the guilty wince."* Quoted in Werhan at 318.

Demosthenes

Such was the Monica Lewinsky sex scandal with President Bill Clinton in 1995. The tabloid press devoted months to the issue, and the mainstream media eventually followed.

journalism today appear tame.[5]

But what type of nation was reading all those newspapers? Was it a Christian nation?

A CHRISTIAN NATION?

Whether this country was founded as a "Christian nation" depends on what you mean by that term.[6]

In fact, it has less to do with history than today's "culture wars."[7]

5. Clinton's was hardly the first sex scandal in America politics. Thomas Jefferson hired a freelance journalist, James T. Callender, to attack Federalists like Alexander Hamilton and John Adams.

In 1797, Jefferson secretly paid Callender to expose Hamilton's affair in 1791 with a banker's wife, Maria Reynolds. The banker, James Reynolds, was arrested for counterfeiting. Hamilton insisted he committed no public misconduct— he only had an affair with Maria Reynolds. After Hamilton left public life he felt compelled to stop rumors of misconduct in office by publishing a detailed confession of his affair. *See* RON CHERNOW, ALEXANDER HAMILTON 529–30 (2004).

Jefferson then turned Callender on Adams. Callender wrote a pamphlet attacking the Federalists called *The Prospect Before Us*. In June 1800, the Adams administration prosecuted Callender under the Sedition Act, and his trial was before Supreme Court Justice Samuel Chase. (The Jeffersonian Republicans later impeached Chase in part for his handling of the Callender trial; *see* WILLIAM H. REHNQUIST, GRAND INQUESTS:

THE HISTORIC IMPEACHMENTS OF JUSTICE SAMUEL CHASE AND PRESIDENT ANDREW JOHNSON (1992)). In addition to a $200 fine, Callender received a jail term under the Sedition Act and was not released until the Adams administration's last day in March 1801. Jefferson pardoned all

journalists, including Callender. Callender then asked Jefferson to appoint him postmaster of Richmond, Virginia. When he did not get the job, he switched sides and began editing the Federalist *Richmond Recorder*. Callender eventually targeted Jefferson, revealing that Jefferson had funded his pamphleteering and published Jefferson's letters to him to prove it. Callender later wrote in a series of articles that Jefferson fathered children by his slave, Sally Hemings. This prompted Adams's wife, Abigail, to comment to Jefferson that the serpent he "*cherished and warmed*" had "*bit the hand that nourished him.*" *Quoted in* DAVID MCCULLOUGH, JOHN ADAMS 577 (2001), and the discussion of the whole incident at 577–85; *see also* REBECCA L. MCMURRY & JAMES F. MCMURRY, JR., THE SCANDALMONGER AND THE NEWSPAPER WAR OF 1802 (2000), with reprints of the newspaper articles of the time detailing the Jefferson/Hemings controversy. Callender drowned on July 17, 1803, in two feet of water in the James River, too drunk to save himself.

A Philosophic Cock by James Akin (c. 1804), showing Jefferson's rooster courting the hen Hemings. The cock was also a symbol of revolutionary France, which Jefferson was known to admire.

6. Scholars argue from two camps: (1) the Founders intended to strictly separate religion from the government; and (2) the Founders were deeply religious people who believed that religion and government should work together. *Compare* Patrick M. Garry, *The Myth of Separation: America's Historical Experience with Church and State*, 33 HOFSTRA L. REV. 475, 476–78 (2004) (the Framers viewed religion as indispensable to government), *with* LAURENCE H. TRIBE, AMERICAN CONSTITUTIONAL LAW §§ 14-3, 14-4 (1978) (the Framers separated church from state for effective government).

7. *See generally* Stone regarding the culture wars. For example, see *Lee v. Weisman*, 505 U.S. 577 (1992), where the Supreme Court outlawed prayers at public school graduations. There are also the nativity scene cases, *Lynch v. Donnelly*, 465 U.S. 668 (1984), and

County of Allegheny v. ACLU, 492 U.S. 573 (1989), where the Supreme Court held against public expression of religious belief.

The Puritans: Certainly, the Puritans were founding a New Jerusalem.[1] Indeed, not just the Puritan colonies were motivated by their relationship with God. The first charter of Virginia, granted by King James I in 1606, was to propagate Christianity, and the other colonies had the same charge.[2]

The Puritans, however, were separatists by definition; they had fled the established government and Church of England. Thus, though the Puritans may have intended both the church and state to be "Godly," they did not necessarily intend to create the type of theocracy in America where the church and the state were the same entity. Though the idea was a "Godly" place on earth, church and state were a check on each other to reach that end.

The Revolutionary Generation: Long before the American Revolution, the Puritan vision proved unattainable. By

---

1. The *Mayflower* Pilgrims came *"for the propagating and advancing the Gospel of the kingdom of Christ in those remote parts of the world."* Tupi at 215, *quoting* WILLIAM BRADFORD, HISTORY OF PLYMOUTH PLANTATION 24 (Little, Brown & Co. 1856).

2. Virginia's 1606 Charter declared: *"[T]o make habitation and to deduce a colony of sundry of our people into that part of America commonly called Virginia in propagating of Christian religion to such people as yet live in darkness."* Tupi at 215, citing 1 HISTORICAL COLLECTIONS: CONSISTING OF STATE PAPERS AND OTHER AUTHENTIC DOCUMENTS: INTENDED AS MATERIALS FOR A HISTORY OF THE UNITED STATES OF AMERICA 50–51 (Ebenezer Hazard ed., T. Dobson 1792).

In *Holy Trinity Church v. United States*, 143 U.S. 457, 465–71 (1892), the Supreme Court traced America's Christian heritage to Christopher Columbus's commission. *Discussed in* Tupi at 211–12. Even John Locke's 1669 Carolina Constitution provided that no man could be a citizen unless he acknowledged God, belonged to a church, and refrained from abusive language against religion. *Id.* at 211–12.

Columbus commissioned to bring God to the New World and get all the gold for Spain that he could lay his paws on

---

3. Stone at 3–5 (*"By the time the Framers began drafting the United States Constitution, church membership had dropped to the point that "not more than one person in . . . ten" was affiliated with a Christian church."*).

The Great Awakenings had a good part to do with the decline of the established churches. These were periods of rapid and dramatic religious revival in Anglo-American religious history beginning in the 1730s. Traveling preachers encouraged many to abandon the established churches for dissenting Protestant sects, causing the established churches to increase

their persecution of religious dissent. Matthew C. Berger, Comment, *One Nation Indivisible: How Congress's Addition of "Under God" to the Pledge of Allegiance Offends the Original Intent of the Establishment Clause*, 3 U. ST. THOMAS L.J. 629, 642 (2006); *see also* BROOKH-

ISER at 27. There were actually several Great Awakenings. Jonathan Edwards (1703–58) and George Whitefield (the cofounder of Methodism, along with John Wesley) were early leaders, and modern evangelical Protestantism traces its roots from them.

the 1770s, American Christianity was in decline, at least the *established* version.[3]

The DECLARATION OF INDEPENDENCE referenced some type of God when it famously declared:

"We hold these truths to be self-evident, that all men are created equal, that they are endowed by their Creator with certain unalienable Rights, that among these are Life, Liberty, and the pursuit of Happiness."[4]

But this God is not a traditional Judeo-Christian God.[5] The "creator" it cites is "Nature's God," who gives "divine providence." This is not the God of Isaac and Jacob, but of Isaac Newton, who demonstrated the universe was knowable because it was rational. It is the Deist God, also called the "Creator," the "First Cause," and the "Grand Architect."

Thus, THE DECLARATION side-stepped Christianity.[6]

---

4. THE DECLARATION OF INDEPENDENCE para. 2 (U.S. 1776). *See* Brookhiser at 60 (discussing the Declaration and Jefferson's *"oblique"* references to God).

5. Stone at 22.

Newton by Blake (1805); man with the instruments of his own construct pierces the darkness

To use an old analogy, it is the "watchmaker God," who set the great clock of the universe in motion for us to discern. Brookhiser at 62. This creator embedded morality and inalienable human rights within nature's laws, and a person could discern them through reason, just like Newton's physics. Stone at 7. Many of our Founding Fathers, including Thomas Paine, Thomas Jefferson, Benjamin Franklin, Ethan Allen, and Gouverneur Morris, were Deists, and many others, including John Adams, James Madison, Alexander Hamilton, James Monroe, and George Washington, were at least partial Deists. Many, such as Patrick Henry, Sam Adams, and John Jay, were traditional Christians. *Id.* at 7–8.

6. Thomas Paine and a "Christian nation." Any modern "Christian nation" proponent must contend with Thomas Paine. Paine's works, COMMON SENSE, THE RIGHTS OF MAN, and THE AGE OF REASON, *"became the three most widely read political tracts of the eighteenth century."* Stone at 21. To the orthodox Christians of his day, and ours, he was *"a villain and an infidel."* Paine declared in THE AGE OF REASON:

"I believe in one God, and no more . . . . I believe in the equality of man; and I believe that religious duties consist in doing justice, loving mercy, and endeavoring to make our fellow-creatures happy. . . . I do not believe in the creed professed by the Jewish Church, by the Roman Church, by the Greek Church, by the Turkish Church, by the Protestant Church, nor by any church that I know of. My own mind is my own church."

Stone at 19–20, *quoting* THOMAS PAINE, THE AGE OF REASON: PART ONE (1794).

In fact, the full title is THE AGE OF REASON; BEING AN INVESTIGATION OF TRUE AND FABULOUS THEOLOGY, which he published in three parts in 1794, 1795, and 1807. Paine certainly had no use for organized religion and wrote that the Christian doctrine of turning the other cheek

Thomas Paine

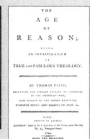

meant *"sinking man into a spaniel." Discussed in* BROOKHISER *at 68–69.* Paine was a Deist who advocated reason in the place of revelation, rejected miracles, and viewed the Bible as ordinary literature. Paine's engaging and irreverent style, as well as his book's inexpensive price, made Deistic ideas available to a mass audience. The fact that he was a best seller in America cuts against the current "Christian nation" argument. Regarding his view on freedom of the press, Paine generally agreed with Blackstone, and in an essay on "Liberty of the Press," he wrote that *"a man does not ask liberty beforehand to say something he has a mind to say, but he becomes answerable afterwards for the atrocities he may utter."* Levy, *Free Press Clause*, at 179.

Compare William Blake's illustration of God as the "Grand Architect" with Michelangelo's traditional image ruling the earth and sky like an old pagan

 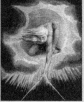

Zeus. Blake's God created the grand watch of the universe symbolized by his compass, the same compass Blake's Newton uses to pierce the darkness.

Franklin, for example, edited Jefferson's original draft that said these truths were *"sacred and undeniable"* to *"self-evident,"* making the clause the document's most moving.[1]

This is not to say the Framers intended to establish an irreligious or anti-Christian nation. Most of them called themselves Christian, even if of a Deist type.[2] And as John Jay noted in

THE FEDERALIST PAPERS, Americans were

"one united people . . . professing the same [Protestant] religion."[3]

Also, the Framers lived in the legal world of the common

---

1. Brookhiser at 60. *See also* Tupi at 203–04 (discussing God in the DECLARATION OF INDEPENDENCE).

2. THE VIRGINIA DECLARATION OF RIGHTS OF 1776 mixed Deism with traditional Christianity: *That religion, or the duty which we owe to our CREATOR, and the manner of discharging it, can be directed only by reason and conviction, not by force or violence; and therefore all men are entitled to free exercise of religion, according to the dictates of conscience; and that it is the mutual duty of all to practice Christian forbearance, love and charity towards each other.* Quoted in Herbert W. Titus, God's Revelation: Foundation for the Common Law, 4 REGENT U. L. REV. 1, 31 (1994). *But see* Tupi at 198 (steadfastly arguing that the Founders were "men of [Christian] faith")

3. THE FEDERALIST No. 2 (John Jay), *quoted in* Brookhiser at 26.

Jay

4. See **Chapter 6 of** *Bills, Quills, and Stills,* **(Constitution Press re-release 2017)** for more on the history of the common law.

5. CATHERINE DRINKER BOWEN, MIRACLE AT PHILADELPHIA: THE STORY OF THE CONSTITUTIONAL CONVENTION, MAY TO SEPTEMBER 1789 63 (1966).

6. See, e.g., Vidal v. Girard's Executors, 43 U.S. 127, 198 (1844) (*"It is also said, and truly, that the Christian religion is a part of the common law."*). *Vidal* followed a long common law history.

For Edward Coke the common law was *"written with the finger of God in the heart of man . . ."* and Moses *"was the first reporter or writer of law in the world."* Quoted in Titus at 2. William Blackstone began his influential COMMENTARIES ON THE LAW OF ENGLAND with the chapter *"The Nature of Laws in General,"* stating the Christian basis of the common law:

Man, considered as a creature, must necessarily be subject to the law of his creator, for he is entirely a dependent being . . . [A] state of dependence will inevitably oblige the inferior to take the will of him, on whom he depends, as the rule of his conduct . . . And consequently, as man depends absolutely upon his maker for everything, it is necessary that he should in all points conform to his maker's will . . . This will of his maker is called the law of nature . . . . Further, law . . . signifies a . . . rule of action, which is prescribed by some superior,

and which the inferior is bound to obey. Quoted in id. at 3. For Blackstone the ultimate "superior" is the traditional Christian God.

Justice Joseph Story later found ample evidence to support the opinion that "[t]here never has been a period, in which the Common Law did not recognise Christianity as lying at its foundations." Quoted in id. at 3. All of this contrasts with THE DECLARATION OF INDEPENDENCE's articulation of "nature's God." But, even Justice William O. Douglas, considered an activist liberal, wrote "[w]e are a religious people whose institutions presuppose a Supreme Being." Zorach v. Clauson, 343 U.S. 306, 313 (1951).

But even before Christianity, humans agreed that law comes from the gods. Shamash, the sun god, handed down edicts to King Hammurabi; Jehovah did the same to Moses, and every nine years Crete's King Minos climbed Mount Olympus to get legal advice from Zeus. KADRI at 3.

Coke

Blackstone

Story

Shamash, the god of the Sun, seated on his throne

Moses bringing down the law

Zeus schooling Minos

law.[4] After all, thirty-five of the fifty-five delegates to the Constitutional Convention were lawyers or judges.[5]

And the common law's basis is Christianity.[6]

In fact, several common-law crimes such as blasphemy and heresy directly reflect Christianity.[7] States were still prosecuting these crimes in the early years of the republic.[8] But, such prosecutions are directly contrary to both freedom of religion and speech. The very existence of a heresy or blasphemy law means that someone is not free to believe or express his or her belief.

Again, the mix of religion and speech is still what it is about.[9]

7. Blackstone devoted another chapter to "*offenses against God and religion,*" where he affirmed the common-law crimes of apostasy, heresy, reviling the ordinances of the church, blasphemy, witchcraft, and Sabbath breaking. Titus at 30.

8. Albert at 37 (noting that blasphemy laws reflected Christianity's infusion into the common law).

Potter Stewart

9. What Is Obscene? Justice Potter Stewart could neither describe obscenity nor hard-core pornography, but famously quipped, "*I know it when I see it . . .*" Jacobellis v. Ohio, 378 U.S. 184, 197 (1964) (Stewart, J., concurring) ("*I shall not today attempt further to define the kinds of material I understand to be embraced within that shorthand description [i.e., "hard-core pornography"]; and perhaps I could never succeed in intelligibly doing so. But I know it when I see it, and the motion picture involved in this case is not that.*"). Jacobellis was about the French film THE LOVERS *(Les Amants)* (Zenith International Films 1958) dealing with adultery and rediscovering love, pretty tame stuff by today's standards, with the Supreme Court holding that the film was not obscene.

Common-law courts were not always the final arbiter of public morality; the Star Chamber and church courts used to do this. But in 1641, the English Parliament did away with the Star Chamber and most of the old church court jurisdiction and gave it to the common-law courts, from which our Supreme Court descends. In a famous case in 1664 Sir Charles Sedley (also spelled "Sidley") got into trouble

for "*having shown his nude body in a balcony in Covent Garden to a great multitude of people, and had said and done certain things to the great scandal of Christianity.*" The Court of King's Bench ruled that it was "*the custos morum ["guardian of morals"] of all the subjects of the King, and it is now high time to punish such profane actions done against all modesty . . .*" Quoted in Berman, *Law and Belief*, at 602. Sedley got a 2,000 mark fine, a week in jail, and three years' probation. Still, Sedley eventually became

Sedley

Speaker of the House of Commons.

As for showing the nude body "*to the great scandal of Christianity*" in America, no laws criminalized pornography at the time of the Bill of Rights. *Roth v. United States*, 354 U.S. 476, 482 (1957). By 1792, though, thirteen of fourteen states prohibited libel and criminalized either blasphemy, profanity, or both. *Id.*; see also Chemerinsky at 903. This is the origin of modern obscenity prosecutions.

Prophets versus Profits. Today, the proponents of obscenity prosecutions are usually conservative religious groups who object to pornography on religious and moral grounds. Thus, they assert their rights under the First Amendment's Free Exercise Clause to fight for their faith. On the other side is the pornography industry and consumer market that relies on the First Amendment's Free Speech Clause to fight for their expression (and profit).

The Framers and Religion: In addition to being part of a Christian culture, the Framers specifically extolled the value and even the necessity of religion.[1]

Our form of government "*required*" a religious people, said John Adams, because

"*our constitution was made only for a moral and religious people. It is wholly inadequate to the government of any other.*"[2]

Indeed,

"*[r]eligion and virtue are the only foundations of republicanism and of all free governments.*"[3]

For Franklin,

"*only a virtuous people are capable of freedom. As nations become corrupt and vicious, they have more need of masters.*"[4]

Franklin also recognized religion's role in sustaining morals:

1. Tupi at 202 (distinguishing between the French "atheistic" revolution and the American one).

Regarding the Founding Fathers' religious beliefs, *see generally* STEVEN WALDMAN, FOUNDING FAITHS: HOW OUR FOUNDING FATHERS FORGED A RADICAL NEW APPROACH TO RELIGIOUS LIBERTY (2009), debunking the myths of both the Christian Right and the secular Left. *See also* GARY KOWALSKI, REVOLUTIONARY SPIRITS: THE ENLIGHTENED FAITH OF AMERICA'S FOUNDING FATHERS (2008); BROOKE ALLEN, MORAL MINORITY: OUR SKEPTICAL FOUNDING FATHERS (2006) (arguing that the Founding Fathers did not establish a "Christian nation"); DAVID L. HOLMES, THE FAITHS OF THE FOUNDING FATHERS (2006); JON MEACHAM, AMERICAN GOSPEL: GOD, THE FOUNDING FATHERS, AND THE MAKING OF A NATION (2007). For the view arguing the Founding Fathers were a species of modern evangelical Christian, *see* TIM F. LAHAYE, FAITH OF OUR FOUNDING FATHERS (1996).

2. Tupi at 255, *quoting* John Adams; *see also* David K. DeWolf, *Ten Tortured Words*, 85 DENV. U. L. REV. 443, 451–52 (2007) (reviewing STEPHEN MANSFIELD, TEN TORTURED WORDS: HOW THE FOUNDING FATHERS TRIED TO PROTECT RELIGION IN AMERICA AND WHAT'S HAPPENED SINCE (2007)).

A young Abigail and John Adams

3. *Quoted in* Tupi at 227.

Adams as a young man, in his 1765 DISSERTATION ON CANON AND FEUDAL LAW, defended the "sensible" New England Puritans against those "*many modern Gentlemen.*" The Puritans were, for Adams, "*illustrious patriots,*" and the first "*to establish a government of the church more consistent with the scriptures, and a government of the state more agreable to the dignity of humane nature than any other seen in Europe: and to transmit such a government down to their posterity.*" Quoted in Witte, City on a Hill, at 41.

But a middle-aged John Adams became increasingly suspicious of religious dogma. As he wrote to Benjamin Rush, "*there is a germ of religion in human nature so strong that whenever an order of men can persuade the people by flattery or terror that they have salvation at their disposal, there can be no end to fraud, violence, or usurpation.*" Quoted in Stone at 13–14. Though a Congregationalist, Adams more closely identified with Unitarianism, a seventeenth century religious movement from England related to Deism. By Adams's time, the English scientist Joseph Priestly was its chief proponent. Adams, Franklin, and Jefferson avidly read Priestly. Id. at 14.

An old John Adams wrote to Jefferson, "*[t]wenty times, in the course of my late Reading, have I been upon the point of breaking out, 'This would be the best of all possible Worlds, if there were no Religion in it'*" but then added

"*[w]ithout Religion this World would be Something not fit to be mentioned in polite Company, I mean Hell.*" Id., quoting Letter from John Adams to Thomas Jefferson (Apr. 19, 1817).

A middle-aged Adams   Adams at 89 (1823)

4. *Quoted in* Tupi at 255.

5. Franklin wrote this to a young friend who had stridently attacked religion, preceding it with the following:
"*You yourself may find it easy to live a virtuous Life without . . . Religion; you . . . possessing a Strength of Resolution sufficient to enable you to resist common Temptations. But think how great a Proportion of Mankind consists of weak and ignorant Men and Women . . . who have need of the Motives of Religion to restrain them from Vice, to support their Virtue, and to retain them in the Practice of it till it becomes habitual. . . . If Men are so wicked as we now see them with Religion what would they be if without it?*" Quoted in Stone at 23–24.

"If Men are so wicked as we now see them with Religion what would they be if without it?" [5]

George Washington believed that religion was useful both to public morality and republican government because

"reason and experience both forbid us to expect that national morality can prevail in the exclusion of religious principle." [6]

Also,

"true religion affords to government its surest support." [7]

Thomas Jefferson did not care if his neighbor believed in twenty gods or no God because

"it neither picks my pocket nor breaks my leg." [8]

Franklin would not pass as a Christian today. He admitted at the end of his life that *"I have . . . some Doubts as to his [Jesus's] Divinity, tho' it is a Question I do not dogmatize upon, [having] never studied it, & think it needless to busy myself with it now, when I expect soon an [opportunity] of [knowing] the Truth with less Trouble."* Stone at 9, citing Letter from Benjamin Franklin to Ezra Stiles (Mar. 9, 1790); see also Brookhiser at 64–65.

"Here is my Creed." Franklin wrote, *"I believe in one God, the Creator of the Universe: That he governs the World by his Providence. That he ought to be worshiped. That the most acceptable Service we can render to him, is doing good to his other Children."* Stone at 8–9.

With an ecumenical nod, Franklin commented that these are *"the fundamental Principles of all sound Religion."* Like Jefferson, Franklin thought Jesus was okay, but that people had corrupted his teachings: *"I think the System of morals & his Religion, as he left them to us, the best the World ever saw or is likely to see; but I apprehend it has received various corrupting changes."*

Invoking his civic-minded God, Franklin called for a prayer each day at the Constitutional Convention and used the invocation of God to smooth the debates. See, e.g., Brookhiser at 62; David L. Wardle, *Reason to Ratify: The Influence of John Locke's Religious Beliefs on the Creation and Adoption of the United States Constitution*, 26 SEATTLE U. L. REV. 291, 301 (2002). John Adams noted that Franklin was a mirror in which people saw their own religion: *"The Catholics thought him almost a Catholic.*

The Church of England claimed him as one of them. The Presbyterians thought him half a Presbyterian, and the Friends believed him a wet Quaker."

If anything, ethics was his religion. When he was twenty years old, in 1726, he listed the thirteen virtues to follow:

1. *"TEMPERANCE. Eat not to dullness; drink not to elevation.*
2. *SILENCE. Speak not but what may benefit others or yourself; avoid trifling conversation.*
3. *ORDER. Let all your things have their places; let each part of your business have its time.*
4. *RESOLUTION. Resolve to perform what you ought; perform without fail what you resolve.*
5. *FRUGALITY. Make no expense but to do good to others or yourself; i.e., waste nothing.*
6. *INDUSTRY. Lose no time; be always employ'd in something useful; cut off all unnecessary actions.*
7. *SINCERITY. Use no hurtful deceit; think innocently and justly, and, if you speak, speak accordingly.*
8. *JUSTICE. Wrong none by doing injuries, or omitting the benefits that are your duty.*
9. *MODERATION. Avoid extremes; forbear resenting injuries so much as you think they deserve.*
10. *CLEANLINESS. Tolerate no uncleanliness in body, cloaths, or habitation.*
11. *TRANQUILLITY. Be not disturbed at trifles, or at accidents common or unavoidable.*
12. *CHASTITY. Rarely use venery but for health or offspring, never to dullness, weakness, or the injury of your own or another's peace or reputation.*
13. *HUMILITY. Imitate Jesus and Socrates."*

Franklin as the homespun American original

6. *Quoted in* Stone at 19.　　**7.** *Quoted in* Tupi at 227.

8. *Quoted in* LEVY, BILL OF RIGHTS, at 108.

Washington

But though Jefferson was at least an agnostic, if not an atheist,[1] he was friendly to most "sectarian" religion for ordering republican life.[2]

More generally, a Frenchman, Alexis de Tocqueville, traveling in America in the early 1800s, noted American religion's role in tempering liberty:

> "[W]hile the law allows the American people to do everything, there are things which religion prevents them from imagining and forbids them to dare."[3]

A Religious People versus a Christian Nation:

When the Framers wrote of the civic value of religion, they generally did so in the context of Protestant Christianity. But that does not necessarily mean they were speaking just of Protestantism or even Christianity.

Most certainly spoke in the context of the religion they knew, Protestant Christianity. But men such as Franklin, and even Washington, showed a broader tolerance. (Or in the case of Jefferson, a broader intolerance of any organized religion, be it Protestant Christianity or anything else!)[4]

Thus, just because the Framers may have recognized religion in society as a stabilizing influence, it does not mean that they intend-

---

1. Jefferson is the secularist's patron saint.

Jefferson cautioned his nephew in 1787 to "shake off all the fears, & servile prejudices under which weak minds are servilely crouched" and to "question with boldness even the existence of a God; because, if there be one, he must more approve of the homage of reason, than that of blindfolded fear." Quoted in Stone at 10. Jefferson, like Washington, did not believe Jesus was divine but that he was the greatest teacher of all time. Id. at 10–11. In fact, Jefferson made his own Bible by cutting and pasting. He removed all sections of the New Testament containing supernatural aspects as well as what he perceived to be misinterpretations that the Four Evangelists had added. Several editions are in print. See, e.g., THOMAS JEFFERSON, THE JEFFERSON BIBLE: THE LIFE AND MORALS OF JESUS OF NAZARETH (2010).

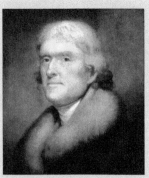

A self-confident and even whimsical Jefferson

2. Tupi at 255. But nothing changed Jefferson's anticlericism and his beliefs regarding the "irritable tribe of priests." BROOKHISER at 72–73. Christian doctrines such as predestination, the inefficacy of good works, and original sin were for Jefferson "nonsense," "dross," "distortions," "abracadabra," "insanity," "demoralizing dogmas," "deliria of crazy imaginations" and "hocus-pocus phantasm." Stone at 11, quoting from various Jefferson letters.

3. Quoted in Tupi at 217.

Alexis deTocqueville

4. As Jefferson once wrote, "I have sworn upon the altar of God eternal hostility against every form of tyranny over the mind of man." Quoted in BROOKHISER at 73.

5. Berger at 648. Martin E. Marty, On a Medial Moraine: Religious Dimensions of American Constitutionalism, 39 EMORY L.J. 9, 13 (1990) ("The Constitution and like documents were not written to save souls, to make sad hearts glad, to build denominational communities or encourage them, to promote public or civic virtue, to invoke God or the gods, or to encourage morality.").

6. Berger at 638.

"Hocus pocus"—Magical conjurors still use this phrase. It most likely comes from "hax pax max Deus adimax," a pseudo-Latin phrase that parodies the Roman Catholic Mass, which contains the phrase "Hoc est enim corpus meum" ("this is the body"). Others believe that it is an appeal to the Norse folklore magician Ochus Bochus or the Welsh "hovea pwca" (a "goblin's trick"). It is also the origin of the word "hoax." HENDRICKSON at 351; AYTO at 284

A 15th century mass

ed to establish a "Christian nation."

The Framers, moreover, specifically created a secular government.[5] They wanted to prevent a Church of the United States similar to the Church of England.[6]

The Constitution, for instance, refers to "*We the People*" as its source of legitimacy, not God:

"*We the People of the United States . . . do*

ordain and establish this Constitution for the United States of America."[7]

The Constitution does twice refer to religion.

The Constitution's first religious reference states it was

"*Done . . . in the Year of our Lord one thousand seven hundred and Eighty seven and of the Indepen- dence of the United States of America the Twelfth.*"[8]

This was a common man- ner of dating documents, which we generally still use today.[9] This way of dating does not change the fact that the Constitution lays out a secular govern- ment, which its second religious reference explic- itly shows:

"*No religious Test shall ever be required as a Qualification to any Office or public Trust under the United States.*"[10]

---

7. Preamble to the Constitution. This contrasts with the constitutions of most of the states, which explicitly recognized religious obligation. Albert at 45.

Regarding the Framers purposefully leaving God out of the Constitution, as compared to the DECLARATION OF INDEPEN- DENCE, see Martin E. Marty, *Freedom of Religion and the First Amendment, in* THE BILL OF RIGHTS: A LIVELY HERITAGE 19 (Jon Kukla ed., 1987).

The Constitutional Convention

The Constitution spells out John Locke's philosophy on government with authority flowing from a social contract be- tween each member of society. Berger at 640–41. Locke, whose writ- ings most directly shaped the intellectual and political worldview of eighteenth century Americans, warned against "*claims to sacred truths.*" Stone at 6–7.

John Locke

8. U.S. CONST. art. VII. The Constitution also excludes Sunday from the day count before a president can veto a bill. Marty, *Freedom of Religion*, at 24.

9. See Marty, *Freedom of Religion*, at 24, arguing "Our Lord" sneaked in only as part of the date. *See also* Berger at 658 n.162 ("in the Year of our Lord" was colonial America's customary way of counting years).

BC and AD: Dionysius Exiguus ("Dennis the Short"), a Scythian monk, introduced "*anno Domini*" ("in the year of the Lord") in about 527. The years following his calculation of Jesus's birth he designated "*anno Domini*" (or "AD"). Thus, all years before we abbreviate as "BC" for "before Christ."

English texts used this system as early as the seventh century. Although modern references include using "CE" ("the common era") and "BCE" ("before the common era"), they are still based on Christ's birth date as the cutoff point. Thus, the old BC and AD system remains current.

Catholic Europe adopted the Gregorian calendar on October 4, 1582, to correct the errors of the then 1,628-year-old

Julian calendar (from Julius Caesar). To fix the problem, the Gregorian calendar took out ten days. Because of England's break with Rome, England did not adopt the Gregorian calendar until 170 years later, in 1753. This is why it is hard to fix the birth date of people like George Washington. But the Gregorian calendar is still what we use today, and is inaccurate only one day every three thousand years. *See* RICH BEYER, THE GREATEST STORIES NEVER TOLD: 100 TALES FROM HISTORY TO ASTONISH, BEWILDER & STU- PEFY 26–27 (2003).

Dennis the Short—or just a monk in a scriptorium?

Pope Gregory XIII

Detail of Pope Gregory's tomb celebrating the Gregorian calendar

10. U.S. CONST. art. VI, cl. 3. Marty, *Freedom of Religion*, at 24, and Tupi at 204–06 note that Article II, Section 1, provides that before taking office, the president "*shall take the following oath or affirmation: — 'I do solemnly swear (or affirm) that I will faithfully execute the office of the President of the United States and will, to the best of my ability, preserve, protect, and defend the Constitution of the United States,*'" and that Article VI, Clause 3, similarly provides that senators and representatives, state legislators, and all executive and judicial officers of the federal and state governments "*shall be bound by oath or affirmation to support this Constitution.*" Although Tupi argues that God is in the "*oath or affirmation,*" this neglects that oaths existed long before we humans had any concept of the Judeo-Christian God. For a brief history of oaths, see **Chapter 5 of Bills, Quills, and Stills, (Constitution Press re-release 2017).**

As we have seen, religious tests went back to Charles II and James II, when Parliament wanted to exclude Catholics from military and public office.[1] The Framers did not want that for America.[2]

The fact that the Constitution does not endorse or even evoke Christianity did not go unnoticed.[3]

In 1789, religious leaders from New England wrote President George Washington *"that the Constitution lacked any reference to the only true God and Jesus Christ, who he hath sent."*[4] Washington replied that *"the path of true piety is so plain as to require but little political direction . . . [only ministers of the gospel could further the] advancement of true religion."*

A unanimous first Senate was even more explicit than Washington about

---

1. American Baptists were vocal proponents of the no religious test clause. Berger at 642.

The distinguished Baptist Reverend Isaac Backus, during the Massachusetts ratifying convention, stated that *"[n]othing is more evident, both in reason and The Holy Scriptures, than that religion is ever a matter between God and individuals; and, therefore, no man or men can impose any religious test without invading the essential prerogatives of our Lord Jesus Christ."* He also stated that *"the imposing of religious tests had been the greatest engine of tyranny in the world."* Id. at 642–43.

Later, Supreme Court Justice Joseph Story explained that Article VI made it possible, on the federal level, for Catholics, Protestants, Calvinists, Jews, and even *"the Infidel, [to] sit down at the common table of the national councils without any inquisition into their faith or mode of worship."* 3 JOSEPH STORY, COMMENTARIES ON THE CONSTITUTION OF THE UNITED STATES 731 (1833).

Backus

Story

2. Berger at 649. According to Maryland delegate Luther Martin, the *"no religious test clause"* was *"adopted by a very great majority of the convention, and without much debate."* James Madison's notes indicate that only one state voted no and one state delegation was divided on the question.

3. The Post Office. Even the Founders had their "culture wars." In the early years of the republic, the nation debated the federal government's secular nature. Congress in 1810 and 1828, despite great pressure from religious groups, required the postal service to work on Sunday. Petitions inundated Congress declaring that the statute made *"it necessary to violate the command of God."* Postal officials countered that frequent mail was essential to the nation's economy and national defense. Congress followed the reasoning that *"[t]he Framers of the Constitution recognized the eternal principle that man's relation with God is above human legislation and his rights of conscience unalienable"* and the federal government lacks the authority to *"define God or point out to the citizen one's religious duty."* New technology eventually eroded the need for Sunday mail service and in 1912 Congress officially closed all Sunday postal service. See Berger at 651. See also Anuj C. Desai, *The Transformation of Statutes into Constitutional Law: How Early Post Office Policy Shaped Modern First*

Persian Empire

Amendment Doctrine, 58 HASTINGS L.J. 671, 673 (2007).

The unofficial Postal Service motto, *"Neither snow nor rain nor heat nor gloom of night stays these couriers from the swift completion of their appointed rounds,"* chiseled in gray granite on the New York City Post Office on 8th Avenue, actually comes from Herodotus's THE PERSIAN WARS (Book 8, ¶ 98). The Persians operated a system of mounted postal couriers who served with great fidelity under that motto. Postal Service Mission and Motto, http://www.usps.com/postalhistory/_pdf/MissionandMotto.pdf#search='motto' (last visited June 12, 2009).

N.Y. City Post Office

the secular American government when it stated in the Tripoli Treaty of 1797 that the United States is

"not, in any sense, founded on the Christian religion" and thus had *"no character of enmity against the laws, religion, or tranquility of Musselmens..."*[5]

The First Amendment followed this secular path:

"Congress shall make no law respecting an establishment of religion...."

At the state level, however, the First Amendment had it detractors. Critics

believed it rejected Christianity and delegates to the state ratifying conventions complained that it would open control of the national government to atheists, Catholics, Jews, and Muslims.

---

4. Berger at 648.

Washington. Which Washington do you want to see? There is the pious one, beseeching God's help during the dark days of Valley Forge.

Washington praying at Valley Forge is a persistent American image despite no documentation that it happened. Some people have this Washington as an article of faith in their Christian America. *See, e.g.,* JANICE CONNELL, FAITH OF OUR FOUNDING FATHER: THE SPIRITUAL JOURNEY OF GEORGE WASHINGTON (2003). But the real Washington spoke as a Deist, referring to *"Providence,"* the *"Almighty Ruler of the Universe,"* the *"Great Architect of the Universe,"* and the *"Great Disposer of Events."* Quoted in Stone at 17–18. According to historian Joseph Ellis, at his death, *"Washington did not think much about heaven or angels; the only place he knew his body was going was into the ground, and as for his soul, its ultimate location was unknowable. He died as a Roman Stoic rather than as a Christian saint."* JOSEPH J. ELLIS, HIS EXCELLENCY: GEORGE WASHINGTON 269 (2004). But one thing is clear; he was a man of tolerance. He said he was *"no bigot myself to any mode of worship."* Stone at 17, quoting George Washington's Letter to Lafayette (Aug. 15, 1787). Indeed, he went beyond mere toleration. To the Jews of the Touro Synagogue he wrote in 1790 that America did not practice *"toleration"* as it was not *"by the indulgence of*

one class of people, that another enjoyed the exercise of their inherent natural rights .... All possess alike liberty of conscience and immunities of citizenship."* Quoted in BROOKHISER at 63. For Washington, toleration was a winning strategy, both for society and the battlefield. In November 1775 Washington barred the *"ridiculous and childish custom of burning the effigy of the Pope"* on Guy Fawkes' Day because it would interfere with attempts to get *"the friendship and alliance of the people of Canada."* Quoted in ALF J. MAPP, THE FAITHS OF OUR FATHERS: WHAT AMERICA'S FOUNDERS REALLY BELIEVED 75 (2005). Washington's order had the effect of ending the practice in America.

English Guy Fawkes Day

Ryan, in first grade, doing a stellar Washington

The English practice was to burn an effigy of Guy Fawkes every November 5. Fawkes conspired to bring back a Catholic monarchy by blowing up King James I and Parliament in the Gunpowder Plot of 1605. England still celebrates it, but now it is generally called "Fireworks Night." In the graphic novel V FOR VENDETTA (1982–89) and the movie V FOR VENDETTA (Warner Brothers. 2005), the main character, V, wears a Guy Fawkes mask.

5. BROOKHISER at 62–63.

"As the government of the United States of America is not in any sense founded on the Christian religion—as it has in itself no character of enmity against the laws, religion, or tranquility of Musselmen [Muslims],— and as the said States never entered into any war or act of hostility against any Mahometan [Islamic] nation, it is declared by the parties that no pretext arising from religious opinions shall ever produce an interruption of the harmony existing between the two countries."

Treaty of Peace and Friendship between the United States of America and the Bey and Subjects of Tripoli of Barbary, art. XI (Nov. 4, 1796), *available at* http://www.yale.edu/lawweb/avalon/diplomacy/barbary/bar1796t.htm (last visited Oct. 14, 2006).

Would any senator today have the courage to vote for such a measure even though our America is far less religious, and more religiously diverse, than the Founders'?

In response, the First Amendment supporters pointed out that it says

"Congress shall make no law . . . ,"

leaving the states free to be as bigoted as ever,[1]

and especially anti-Catholic.[2]

Most of the new states, in fact, had established—meaning state-supported—churches. Although the American colonies

themselves were formally under the Church of England, colonial charters, religious dissent, and the Atlantic Ocean allowed diversity.

The northern states generally favored Puritanism

---

1. *See* Tupi at 209, noting that the First Amendment's main purpose was to only restrain the federal government from establishing a national religion. Justice Story confirmed that the First Amendment left the whole subject of religion exclusively to the states. STORY at 731.

2. **Anti-Catholicism: As American as Apple Pie!** Americans did not like Catholics. Given the fact that not many were around in colonial America, this tells a lot about cultural prejudice. *See, e.g.,* BROOKHISER at 17, 26 (in 1785 Catholics were less than 1 percent of the population, numbering only approximately 24,500). The fact is that all the states but Virginia had religious tests to disqualify those of nonestablished faiths, especially Catholics.

- THE DECLARATION OF INDEPENDENCE indicted King George III for upholding the rights of Catholic Canadians: *"He has . . . abolish[ed] the free [Protestant] system of English laws in a neighboring province."* This is ironic because both George III and George IV opposed Catholic emancipation in England. LOVELL at 417.
- **John Adams,** an enlightened and educated man, wrote his wife Abigail regarding Catholicism: *"Here is everything which can lay hold of the eye, ear and imagination. Everything*

which can charm and bewitch the simple and ignorant. I wonder how Luther ever broke the spell." Quoted in BROOKHISER at 26.

- **Benedict Arnold** justified his treason because of America's alliance with Catholic France, *"the enemy of the Protestant faith."* *Id.* at 17. (How much this had to do with Washington favoring French General Lafayette over him is an open question.)
- **Milton** traced all the evils of licensing and censorship to Roman Catholicism. It was the Vatican's 1418 campaign to suppress Wycliffe and Huss, precursors of the Reformation, that started systematic censorship, with this culminating after the Reformation in the Council of Trent and Spanish Inquisition. For Milton, Catholics did not get the toleration he preached for others because they had nothing to contribute to spiritual truth ; he said that one thing *"we know"* is the utter falsity of the *"teachings of the Roman Catholic faith."* In his earlier writings, Milton hinted vaguely that the class of heretics included Jews, Muslims, *"atheists"* and those given to *"popery, and open superstition."* By 1659 he had narrowed the list to just one: *"the papist only; he is the only heretic,"* for he *"counts all heretics but himself."* Catholicism is not so much *"a religion, but a Roman principality."*

Quoted in Witte, *Milton,* at 1569–70.

- **Locke** advocated in his Letter Concerning Toleration (1689) that every person *"has the supreme and absolute authority of judging for himself"* in matters of faith. Everyone that is but Catholics, Muslims, and other believers *"who deliver themselves up to the service and protection of another prince."* Locke was also intolerant of *"those . . . who deny the being of a God"* for *"promises, covenants, and oaths which are the bonds of human society, can have no hold upon an atheist."* Witte, Milton, at 1603–04.
- **Blackstone** justified treating Catholics as second-class citizens under the law because of their allegiance to the Pope: *"As to papists, what has been said of the Protestant dissenters would hold equally strong for a general toleration of them; provided their separation was founded only upon difference of opinion in religion, and their principles did not also extend to a subversion of the civil government. If once they could be brought to renounce the supremacy of the pope, they might quietly enjoy their seven sacraments, their purgatory, and auricular confession; their worship of reliques and images; nay even their transubstantiation. But while they acknowledge a foreign power, superior to the sovereignty of the kingdom, they cannot complain*

Adams

Arnold

Milton

Locke

Blackstone

(later Congregationalism) and the southern states Anglicanism (later Episcopalianism).[3]

State governments supported the established clergy from taxes that everyone had to pay, regardless of faith.[4] Taxes also supported church buildings.[5]

One thing to keep in mind, however, is that churches were the main social service agencies of their day. Today we expect government to provide and support our hospitals, orphanages, poor houses, and social welfare.[6] We also view public education as a constitutional and secular right.[7] In the Framers' world, churches did these things.[8]

if the laws of that kingdom will not treat them upon the footing of good subjects." 4

WILLIAM BLACKSTONE, COMMENTARIES *54. DeWolf at 452. But one example in English law is that the Toleration Act of 1689 applied to Protestant nonconformists (mostly Puritans) but not Catholics, ironic because Catholics are theologically closer to Anglicans than Puritans. LOVELL at 400. The English colonials brought their anti-Catholicism to America, which flourished to the point of costing Al Smith the presidency in 1928 against Herbert Hoover and was still an issue in John F. Kennedy's election.

Smith   Hoover   Kennedy

3. Berger at 633–34 (noting that nine of the thirteen colonies had some form of established religion by the Revolution); see also Tupi at 209–10; Marty, *Freedom of Religion*, at 20.

4. See Witte, *Tax Exemption*, at 371 (these taxes included "tithe rates" to meet general ecclesiastical expenses and "church rates" to maintain church property. Nonconformists, usually Baptists, Quakers, Catholics, and Jews still had to pay the taxes.

A modern argument is that public education is religion and that
™No one in America would require an atheist or agnostic to pay taxes to support the church or the church school. Yet millions of American Christians are required to pay for an educational program that assumes that there is no God, or that, if He exists, He is irrelevant to history, science, and language. American school children study subjects as if the Author of these subjects does not even exist."
Titus at 35. See also ANN COULTER, GODLESS: THE CHURCH OF LIBERALISM (2006) (arguing that liberalism is a religion that seeks to supplant "traditional" Christianity).

5. Boston's Old North Church.

6. In 1935, the Social Security Administration was the first major federal welfare agency.

7. Regarding the role of churches in education see LEVY, BILL OF RIGHTS, at 97–98, discussing Article III of the Massachusetts Declaration of Rights.

On the national level, Congress appropriated money to pay for missionaries among the Native Americans, mostly for educational reasons. Berger at 650. The Northwest Ordinance in 1789 explicitly encouraged schools in the territory to teach "religion, morality, and knowledge." Tupi at 225.

8. The founders of two of the oldest America universities, Harvard (1636) and Yale (1701), intended them to be Christian. The 1636 Harvard University rules declared: "Let every student be plainly instructed and earnestly pressed to consider well the main end of his life and studies is to know God and Jesus Christ which is eternal life (John 17:3) and therefore to lay Christ in the bottom as the only foundation of all sound knowledge and learning."

Yale's rules of 1787 declared: "All the scholars are required to live a religious and blameless life according to the rules of God's Word, diligently reading the holy Scriptures, that fountain of Divine light and truth, and constantly attending all the duties of religion. All the scholars are obliged to attend Divine worship in the College Chapel on the Lord's Day and on Days of Fasting and Thanksgiving appointed by public Authority."

Quoted in Tupi at 216–17; see also BROOKHISER at 18.

Dissenters from the established churches suffered civil disabilities, such as exclusion from universities and/or disqualification from office.[1]

Often though, especially in New England, states supported multiple established churches,[2] breaking from the European tradition.[3] At the time, one could speak of Lutheran Sweden, Anglican England, Catholic Spain, and Presbyterian Scotland, but no one church for America.[4]

America was, after all, a land of dissenters. We still cherish the image of the lonely Pilgrims who fled the Old World for freedom and opportunity.[5]

True, most of the dissenters were intolerant when they got here. But especially by the Revolution, enough conflicting dissenters led to toleration.[6]

In Virginia, for instance, men like Jefferson, Madison, and Washington did not believe the state should force people to support a church.[7] Both Jefferson's Statute for Religious Freedom and the Virginia Declaration of Rights allowed for real toleration and ended the state's established religion.[8]

This was Madison's background when he prepared the drafts of the Bill of Rights, most especially the First Amendment.[9]

---

1. Levy, Bill of Rights, at 90. Virginia passed laws in the late 1600s, for example, that prohibited Quakers from assembling. Also, non-Anglican preachers had to get a special license to preach. Between 1765–78, Virginia jailed forty-five Baptist ministers for not getting the license. Tupi at 209–10.

2. For variations of the establishment formula in the colonies, see Levy, Bill of Rights, at 97. Generally, the New England colonies adopted a system of multiple local establishments. New York, for example, had a dual establishment of the Anglican and Dutch churches. Berger at 633–34. Massachusetts maintained an established church but endorsed the principle of no preference, allowing for other churches to freely exercise their faith. Levy, Bill of Rights, at 83. See also John Witte, Jr., "A Most Mild and Equitable Establishment of Religion": John Adams and The Massachusetts Experiment, 41 J. Church & St. 213 (1999).

3. Levy, Bill of Rights, at 101. See also Levy, Bill of Rights, at 91, noting that American establishment was never as bad (i.e., discriminatory) as in Europe.

Colonial Maryland

5. Pilgrims landing on Plymouth Rock.

4. But, even in more tolerant America, no colony ever established (i.e., supported) all religions without exception. They always supported Protestantism or at most Christianity—no Judaism, Buddhism, Hinduism, Islam ("Mohammadism"), or any other "ism"!
   Maryland used the term "Christian" religion to be established rather than "Protestant," to allow for its Catholic population. Levy, Bill of Rights, at 99. Maryland was actually founded as a Catholic colony.

6. The Declaration of Independence triggered gradual disestablishment, and the Bill of Rights accelerated the trend. See Albert at 23–24 regarding the disestablishment of religion in the various colonies/states, noting that four colonies in 1776, and one each in 1777 and 1786, had disestablished religion. Establishment did not end until 1818 in Connecticut and 1833 in Massachusetts. Marty, Freedom of Religion, at 21; Levy, Bill of Rights, at 98. Massachusetts being the last may have been due to the relatively tolerant nature of its establishment to begin with.

7. Marty, Freedom of Religion, at 20. See also Berger at 647, noting that Virginia adopted the Lockean perspective on religious freedom, as demonstrated in Madison's Memorial and Remonstrance against Religious Assessments.

8. To get it through the Virginia House of Burgesses, Madison had to help Patrick Henry become governor. This got Henry out of the legislature, which opened the way for the Declaration of Rights, allowing for religious toleration. Marty, Freedom of Religion at 21. See also Levy, Bill of Rights at 85–86, noting most of the Founders, especially Madison, thought established religion not good and that he believed in the high wall of separation of church and state. Regarding Madison's Memorial and Remonstrance against Religious Assessments and the Virginia General Assessment Bill of 1784, see Levy, Bill of Rights at 85.

MADISON AND HIS FIRST AMENDMENT

The First Amendment was Madison's special project.[10] It was, in fact, his progeny, and though not initially all he wanted, it grew into itself.

Madison believed in individual conscience and the right to express it. Thus, the First Amendment embodies not only the free exercise and anti-establishment of religion, but also freedom of speech and press.[11]

In 1789, most of the Constitutional Convention delegates thought explicitly protecting speech and religion unnecessary.[12] As Alexander Hamilton argued in THE FEDERALIST No. 84,

"[w]hy should it be said that the liberty of the press shall not be restrained, when no power is given by which restrictions may be imposed."[13]

History showed Hamilton's argument unpersuasive.

The original Constitution's lack of a Bill of Rights left Madison having to contend with a very powerful Patrick Henry during the Virginia ratifying convention.[14] To win his seat in Congress, Madison agreed to champion a Bill of Rights, including what is now the First Amendment.

---

9. All of this disestablishment gave us English's reputed longest word and a spelling bee favorite: "antidisestablishmentarianism." (Two good movies revolving around spelling bees are BEE SEASON (Fox Searchlight PICTURES 2005) and AKEELAH AND THE BEE (Lionsgate 2006).)

The word actually means going against religion's disestablishment back to establishment. Thus you could say antidisestablishmentarianism is contrary to the First Amendment's anti-establishment clause.

Antidisestablishmentarianism originated in nineteenth century Britain against disestablishing the Church of England. The word has 28 letters and 12 syllables.

10. Marty, *Freedom of Religion*, at 19.

11. *See* O'Brien at 44–46, and LEVY, BILL OF RIGHTS, at 118, noting Madison's original 1789 proposal went well beyond Blackstone to protect the free press.

12. Charles Pinckney of South Carolina proposed *"that the liberty of the Press should be inviolably observed."* Roger Sherman replied, *"It is unnecessary. The Power of Congress does not extend to the Press."* Quoted in Leonard W. Levy, *Bill of Rights in* ESSAYS ON THE MAKING OF THE CONSTITUTION 258, 259 (Leonard W. Levy ed., 1987). Also, all agreed that the federal government had no power over religion. LEVY, BILL OF RIGHTS, at 81, 83–84 (listing several of the Founders on this point).

13. In fact, Hamilton argued, writing it down just invites encroachment because *"[w]ho can give it any definition which would not leave the utmost latitude for evasion?"* Ultimately, Hamilton contended, *"its security . . . must altogether depend on public opinion."*

THE FEDERALIST No. 84 (Alexander Hamilton), *discussed in* O'Brien at 45; *see also* THE FEDERALIST No. 51 (James Madison) (discussion of religion). Hamilton's excuses regarding the lack of a Bill of Rights did not satisfy the Anti-Federalists. *See, e.g.,* Thomas B. McAffee, *The Bill of Rights, Social Contract Theory, and the Rights "Retained" by the People*, 16 S. ILL. U. L.J. 267, 278 (1992) (noting that among the natural rights the Anti-Federalists were most anxious to protect was freedom of the press).

Alexander Hamilton

14. Regarding Madison's debates with Henry during the Virginia ratifying convention and how Madison's arguments disarmed Henry and allowed for Virginia to ratify the Constitution, see Gregory C. Downs, *Religious Liberty That Almost Wasn't: On the Origin of the Establishment Clause of the First Amendment*, 30 U. ARK. LITTLE ROCK L. REV. 19 (2007).

Roger Sherman   Charles Pinckney

James Madison

Patrick Henry

Regarding religion, Madison's first draft of June 8, 1789, read:

> *"The civil rights of none shall be abridged on account of religious belief or worship, nor shall any national religion be established, nor shall the full and equal rights of conscience be in any manner, or on any pretext, infringed."*[1]

Through the legislative process, this eventually became the First Amendment.[2]

Madison also wanted the First Amendment to apply to the states. But what Congress wanted was a guarantee that the federal government would not impose a national religion.[3] Congress was more interested in protecting

each state's right to establish its own religion than in protecting freedom of religion itself.[4]

Given the thinking at the time regarding the First Amendment, we can only now look at what most of the Framers wanted as nascent. They gave us a First Amendment that had the potential to be

---

1. Berger at 635–36, *citing* 1 ANNALS OF CONG. at 451. *See* LEVY, BILL OF RIGHTS, at 86–87 (regarding Congress and especially the Senate defeating Madison's original motion).

2. Responding to criticism that his draft would harm religion, Madison responded with the thinking of Milton and Locke that he "*apprehended the meaning of the words to be, that Congress should not establish a religion, and enforce the legal observation of it by law, nor compel men to worship God in any manner contrary to their conscience.*" Berger at 636, *citing* 1 ANNALS OF CONG. at 758.

3. Berger at 645–46, noting that while debating proposed constitutional amendments, Congress considered and rejected an amendment applying many of the First Amendment protections to the states:
> "*No State shall infringe the equal rights of conscience, nor the freedom of speech or of the press, nor of the right of trial by jury in criminal cases.*"
1 ANNALS OF CONG. at 783. The intent was to leave these matters to the states. LEVY, BILL OF RIGHTS, at 119; Marty, *Freedom of Religion*, at 24–25; *see also* Albert at 6.

4. The same was true for the press, where the First Amendment originally reserved to the states the authority to legislate speech and press. Levy, *Free Press Clause*, at 207. *See also* Rutland at 35–38 (outlining early state bill of rights guarantees of free press, especially Virginia's). *Gitlow v. New York*, 268 U.S. 652, 666 (1925), finally held that freedom of the press is protected from state interference under the Fourteenth Amendment's Due Process Clause. *See* Rutland at 39.

5. The Establishment Clause Today. The original intent of the 1789 Convention does not today control our reading of the First Amendment. Instead, the original intent of the Congress and people that passed the Fourteenth Amendment controls. *See* **Epilogue: How We Ponied Up to Pay the Bill.** In *Everson v. Board of Education*, 330 U.S. 1, 15–16 (1947), Justice Hugo Black for the Supreme Court defined the modern Establishment Clause:
> "*The 'establishment of religion' clause of the First Amendment means at least this: Neither a state nor the Federal Government can set up a church. Neither can pass laws which aid one religion, aid all religions, or prefer one religion over another. Neither can force nor influence a person to go to or to remain away from church against his will or force him to profess a belief or disbelief in any religion. No person can be punished for entertaining or professing religious beliefs or disbeliefs, for church attendance or non-attendance. No tax in any amount, large or small, can be levied to support any religious activities or institutions, whatever they may be called, or whatever they may adopt to teach or practice religion. Neither a state nor the Federal Government can, openly or secretly, participate in the affairs of any religious organizations or groups and vice versa. In the words of Jefferson, the clause against establishment of religion by law was intended to erect 'a wall of separation between Church and State.'*"

Hugo Black

See Berger at 654; Albert at 14. Justice William Rehnquist, dissenting in *Wallace v. Jaffree*, 472 U.S. 38 (1985), a case striking down a state law requiring "*silent meditation or voluntary prayer,*" argued *Everson* was flawed because "*[t]he Establishment Clause did not require governmental neutrality between religion and irreligion nor did it prohibit the federal government from providing nondiscriminatory aid to religion.*" Discussed in LEVY, BILL OF RIGHTS, at 80.

6. The Establishment Clause's Evolution. A philosopher of religion would probably say whether God exists has nothing to do with *how* God chose to create man and nature. This is basically the Catholic Church's position. *See Dogma*, THE CATHOLIC ENCYCLOPEDIA, http://www.newadvent.org/cathen/05089a.htm (last visited Nov. 12, 2009). Despite this, Creationism seems to make God's existence contingent on disproving Darwinism.

The 1926 Scopes Monkey Trial, *State v. Scopes*, 152 Tenn. 424 (Tenn. 1925), *Scopes v. State*, 278 S.W. 57 (Tenn. 1925), tested the Butler Act, which made it unlawful in any Tennessee state-funded school and university "*to teach any theory that denies the story of the Divine Creation of man as taught in the Bible, and to teach instead that man has descended from a lower order of animals.*" In reality it was a staged presentation for the controversy

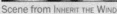
Scene from INHERIT THE WIND

what Madison wanted all along.[5]

And what he wanted was for America to separate church and state.[6]

THE "WALL" SEPARATING CHURCH AND STATE

Nowhere does the Constitution or Bill of Rights say "separation of church and state." But the principle is the way the Supreme Court has worked out how the First Amendment's Establishment and Free Exercise Clauses function together.[7] The concept makes the United States the first society to separate church and state.[8]

Jefferson gets credit for the phrase "the wall of separation of church and state" and thus our modern law on the subject.[9] Jefferson responded to the Danbury Baptist Association of Connecticut in 1802, which suggested that he declare a day of fasting for national reconciliation following his bitter political campaign against Adams:

---

culminating in Clarence Darrow's cross-examination of William Jennings Bryant and tripping him up on the Bible's inconsistencies. The film INHERIT THE WIND (United Artists 1960) culminates in this exchange and was really about McCarthyism. The play's title comes from Proverbs 11:29: "He that troubleth his own house shall inherit the wind."

   Creation science attempts to support the Bible's account of creation and disprove accepted scientific theories about the Earth's history. Fundamentalist Christians are its most vocal proponents, advocating that it be taught in public schools.

   In Epperson v. Arkansas, 393 U.S. 97 (1968), the Supreme Court invalidated an Arkansas law that prohibited teaching evolution in public schools because "teaching and learning must [not] be tailored to the principles or prohibitions of any religious sect or dogma."
Later the federal judge in McLean v. Arkansas Board of Education, 529 F. Supp. 1255, 1258–64 (E.D. Ark. 1982), held that the Arkansas Balanced Treatment for Creation-Science and Evolution-Science Act violated the Establishment Clause. In Edwards v. Aguillard, 482 U.S. 578 (1987), the Supreme Court ruled that a Louisiana law requiring the teaching of creation science along with evolution unconstitutionally sought to advance a particular religion. Supporting Aguillard were seventy-two Nobel prize-winning scientists, seventeen state academies of science, and seven other scientific organizations, describing creation science as religious.

Darwin as "A Venerable Orangoutang" (1871)

Darrow and Bryant

7. In Everson v. Board of Education, 330 U.S. 1, 18 (1947), the question was whether a local school board could reimburse parents, including some with children in Catholic schools, for costs of transportation. Justice Hugo Black wrote,

"the First Amendment has erected a wall between church and state. That wall must be kept high and impregnable. We could not approve the slightest breach."

Separating Church and State in Concord, New Hampshire

8. Marty, Freedom of Religion, at 20.
   In the United States we use the word "minister" to refer to a religious person, usually clergy, who performs functions or services such as teaching, weddings, baptisms, or funerals. In other countries a "minister" can be a government official, such as the British prime minister. Americans use the term "secretary" for these functions, as in secretary of state. "Minister" comes from a Middle English phrase, from the Old French "ministre," originally "minister" in Latin, meaning "servant."

Prime Minister Winston Churchill

9. Barbara A. Perry, Jefferson's Legacy to the Supreme Court: Freedom of Religion, 31 SUP. CT. HIST. 181 (2006). Starting with the first significant Establishment Clause case in the nineteenth century, Reynolds v. United States, 98 U.S. 145 (1878), the Supreme Court pointed to Jefferson as "an acknowledged leader of the advocates of [the Establishment Clause]," and then went on to say that his views "may be accepted as authoritative declaration of the scope and effect of the [Establishment Clause]." But see Mark J. Chadsey, Thomas Jefferson and the Establishment Clause, 40 AKRON L. REV. 623 (2007) (documenting and arguing that Jefferson's thinking had little or no effect on the Establishment Clause's adoption). See also John Witte, Jr., Book Review, 16 J.L. & RELIGION 565 (2001) (reviewing DANIEL L. DREISBACH, RELIGION AND POLITICS IN THE EARLY REPUBLIC: JASPER ADAMS AND THE CHURCH-STATE DEBATE (1996)) (discussing Jasper Adams (1793–1841) of South Carolina as an exponent of a typical early nineteenth century American view of religious liberty that was not Jeffersonian).

"Believing with you that religion is a matter which lies solely between man and his God . . . I contemplate with sovereign reverence that act of the whole American people which declared that their legislature should 'make no law respecting an establishment of religion, or prohibiting the free exercise thereof,' thus building a wall of separation between Church and State." [1]

Jefferson was a good writer; thus, he did what most good writers do and stole metaphors from others, in this case the *"wall of separation."* [2]

Jefferson probably stole it from Roger Williams. In 1643, Williams called for *"a wall of separation between the garden of the Church and the wilderness of the world."* [3] In his case the wall of separation was to protect religion, not necessarily government. [4]

But Jefferson may have also stolen the *"wall of separation"* metaphor from Milton and Locke.

For Milton, the mixing of government and religious power was *"a whoredom"*:

"[S]uffer[ing] the two powers, the ecclesiastical and the civil, which are so totally distinct, to commit whoredom together, and, by their intermingled and false riches, to strengthen indeed in appearance, but in reality to undermine, and at last to subvert one another." [5]

Locke closely tracked Milton regarding religious liberty:

"The care therefore of every man's soul belongs unto himself, and is to be left unto himself." [6]

Because of this, the state has no more business trying to care for a man's soul than it has in trying to prevent him from neglecting his finances. For a man to care for his own soul, it was crucial that the church be *"absolutely separate and distinct from the commonwealth . . ."*

---

1. *Quoted in* Berger at 649 n.125 (added emphasis); *discussed in* Berger at 634–35 and 649–50. Ironically, Adams believed the same as Jefferson about the separation of church and state. *"Nothing,"* he wrote Benjamin Rush, *"is more dreaded than the national government meddling with religion . . . . I mix religion with politics as little as possible."* When a clergyman entered Congress, Adams wrote his wife Abigail that *"as he is the first gentleman of the cloth who has appeared in Congress, I cannot but wish he may be the last. Mixing the sacred character with that of the statesman . . . is not attended with any good effects."* Quoted in Stone at 15.

John Adams

2. Regarding metaphors, Jefferson would have known that Aristotle wrote *"the greatest thing by far is to be a master of metaphor . . . since a good metaphor implies an intuitive perception of the similarity in dissimilars."* ARISTOTLE, POETICS 1459a (McGill–Queen's University Press 1997).

3. *Quoted in* Witte, *Milton*, at 1573; see also Berger at 639–40.

4. The Wall Protecting Religion. Roger Williams cofounded the Baptist faith in America, though he left that church only a few months later. Today, Baptists and Evangelicals often push for more government support of religion. Secularists conversely look with distrust on programs like President George W. Bush's White House Office of Faith-Based Initiatives.

But for most of the Framers, the wall between church and state was not to protect government but to protect religion *from* the government. See Marty, *Freedom of Religion*, at 24; LEVY, BILL OF RIGHTS, at 86–88; Downs *generally* (noting the role of the Virginia Baptist leader John Leland in establishing religious freedom); Berger at 643; Robert A. Sedler, *Essay: The Protection of Religious Freedom under the American Constitution*, 53 WAYNE L. REV. 817 (2007) (noting the overriding purpose of the religion clauses is to protect religious freedom). The Founders' concerns are as relevant today. *See, e.g.,* Douglas Laycock, *"Noncoercive" Support for Religion: Another False Claim about the Establishment Clause*, 26 VAL. U. L. REV. 37, 69 (1992) (*"Government by its sheer size, visibility, authority, and pervasiveness could profoundly affect the future of religion in America. For government to affect religion in this way is for government to change religion, to distort religion, to interfere with religion. Government's preferred form of religion is theologically and liturgically thin. It is politically compliant, and supportive of incumbent administrations."*).

FAITH-BASED AND COMMUNITY INITIATIVES

ROGER WILLIAMS

5. *Quoted in* Witte, *Milton*, at 1562–63. Milton often returned to this theme, calling it *"absurd"* that Christians have *"not learned to distinguish rightly between civil power and ecclesiastical."* The Bible makes clear that *"Christ's kingdom is not of this world,"* and his church *"does not stand by force or constraint, the constituents of worldly authority."* Id. at 1563. Also, *"the combining of ecclesiastical and political government . . . is equally destructive to both . . . ."* Id. at n.147.

Milton

Locke was important for the founding generation, especially Jefferson.[7] So when Jefferson was looking for a source for the metaphor regarding the "wall of separation," among Williams, Milton, and Locke he had plenty from which to choose.

SYMBOLS OF RELIGION AND SPEECH

People have always used symbols to make a statement,[8] especially in the context of religious and political expression.[9] America at the time of the Framers was no different. For example,

- Colonists burned the pope in effigy during "Pope Day" (still called Guy Fawkes Day in England).

- Protesting the Stamp Act, colonists placed various effigies on a "Liberty Tree" (a large elm), including a devil looking out of a boot, which was a pun on the name of British Prime Minister Lord Bute (pronounced "Boot") who the colonists (erroneously) thought was responsible for the Stamp Act.

- After the Declaration of Independence, Americans burned King George III's effigy, emblems, portrait, and coat of arms. Later, they burned effigies of unpopular governors and people like John Jay, coauthor of THE FEDERALIST PAPERS and Supreme Court Chief Justice, for negotiating the much opposed treaty with England.

- Englishmen and Americans honored John Wilkes for his printing *The North Britain* No. 45, with forty-five toasts at political dinners where forty-five diners ate forty-five pounds of beef. At other dinners, the meal was "*eaten from plates marked 'No. 45.'*" Colonists also thinned out Boston's Liberty Tree to forty-five branches.[10]

---

6. Locke went on:
"*But what if he neglect the care of his soul? I answer, what if he neglect the care of his health, or of his estate; which things are nearlier [sic] related to the government of the magistrate than the other? Will the magistrate provide by an express law, that such an [sic] one shall not become poor or sick? Laws provide, as much as is possible, that the goods and health of subjects be not injured by the fraud or violence of others; they do not guard them from the negligence or ill husbandry of the possessors themselves. No man can be forced to be rich or healthful, whether he will or no.*" JOHN LOCKE, *A Letter Concerning Toleration, in* TWO TREATISES OF GOVERNMENT AND A LETTER CONCERNING TOLERATION 227–28 (Ian Shapiro ed., 2003); *quoted in* Toll at 421.

John Locke

7. *See* Berger at 640 (discussing Locke's influence on the American Constitution). *See generally* Wardle (discussing both Locke's deep personal Christian faith, belief in religious tolerance, and influence on America's Founders).

8. Death by crucifixion was a Roman symbol of political power. Christians made it a symbol of faith, depicted millions of times from the ornate Calvary scenes to the simple cross.

Calvary by Paolo Veronese (16th century)

10. *See* Eugene Volokh, *Symbolic Expression and the Original Meaning of the First Amendment*, 97 GEO. L.J. 1057, 1061 (2009) (discussing the various examples of symbolic speech during the Framer's era).

9. The symbols abound, from variations between sects, such as the Eastern Orthodox cross to the symbols of different religions and political movements: the Jewish star of David, the Taoist yin and yang, the Islamic star and crescent, the Hindi swastika to the Nazi swastika and the Communist sickle and hammer. Symbols used together can be symbols of a political statement, such as variations of the popular "COEXIST" bumper sticker.

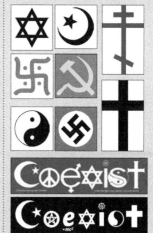

If this history shows anything, it is that symbols have been powerful speech in America.[1]

People pray and pledge not only to what the symbols represent but to the symbols themselves.[2]

Almost by definition, their purposeful desecration or destruction is a statement and speech[3]—

perhaps ugly and bigoted, but *speech* nonetheless.[4]

THE FIRST AMENDMENT AS YOUR PERSONAL SAVIOR

Religion and speech are a powerful combination:

"But when men have realized that time has upset many fighting faiths, they may come to believe . . . that the best test of truth is the power of the thought to get itself accepted in the competition of the market . . . . That at any rate is the theory of our constitution."[5]

So wrote Justice Oliver Wendell Holmes, and his marketplace of ideas metaphor guides the

---

1. "It's a Grand Old Flag/ A High Flying Flag!" Federal law, 36 U.S.C. § 301, attempts to preserve the symbolic power of the American flag by specifying conduct during the national anthem—hand held over heart, etc. Thus, the American flag itself is *speech*; coupled with the "Star Spangled Banner," it makes a powerful statement.

The flag during the War of 1812

Surviving 1814 broadside of the "Defense of Fort McHenry," Francis Scott Key's poem that later became the "Star Spangled Banner"

A fifteen-star, fifteen-stripe "Star Spangled Banner"

---

2. "*I pledge allegiance to the flag*" is how millions of America school children begin their day. When Francis Bellamy wrote it as a children's recitation for the 400th anniversary of Columbus's discovery of America, it originally had no reference to either God or the United States: "*I pledge allegiance to my Flag, and to the Republic for which it stands: one Nation indivisible, With Liberty and Justice for all.*"

In 1923 and 1924, the National Flag Conference claimed that immigrants would confuse the words "*my Flag*" for the flag of their native land and consequently added "*of the United States of America.*" It was not until 1942 that Congress even recognized the Pledge of Allegiance. Berger at 631.

As for "*under God,*" on April 22, 1951, the Catholic Knights of Columbus added it for its organization's meetings, and a year later called for Congress to insert it into the pledge. Congress did so in 1954, citing other examples of religion in American

Original Pledge Salute (Bellamy Salute) of the Pledge of Allegiance.

history, including the 1620 Mayflower Compact, the 1776 Declaration of Independence, President Abraham Lincoln's 1863 Get-

tysburg Address, and the 1864 inscription of "In God We Trust" on American coins. Such a reference, Congress asserted, distinguished America from "*the atheistic and materialistic concepts of communism with its attendant subservience of the individual.*" Berger at 632, *citing* H.R. Rpt. 83-1693; Sen. Rpt. 83-1313. This amendment brought the pledge to the form we know today:

"*I pledge allegiance to the Flag of the United States of America, and to the Republic for which it stands, one Nation under God, indivisible, with liberty and justice for all.*" 4 U.S.C. § 4 (2000). When President Eisenhower signed the change into law on June 14, 1954, he declared:

"*From this day forward, the millions of our school children will daily proclaim in every city and town, every village and rural school house, the dedication of our nation and our people to the Almighty . . . . In this way we are reaffirming the transcendence of religious faith in America's heritage and future; in this way we shall constantly strengthen those spiritual weapons which forever will be our country's most powerful resource in peace or in war.*" Berger at 633.

It shocked many when in June 2002 the U.S. Court of Appeals for the Ninth

Circuit, in *Newdow v. U.S. Congress (Newdow I),* 292 F.3d 597 (9th Cir 2002), held the 1954 statute unconstitutional. The Senate unanimously denounced the decision, President George W. Bush dubbed it "*ridiculous,*" House Minority Whip Tom DeLay called it "*sad*" and "*absurd,*" Senate Majority Leader Tom Daschle referred to it as "*nuts,*" and Senator Robert Byrd of West Virginia called the judges "*stupid.*" See William Trunk, *The Scourge of Contextualism: Ceremonial Deism and the Establishment Clause,* 49 B.C. L. Rev. 571 (2008). Congress reaffirmed the pledge with "*under God.*" Pub. L. No. 107-293, 116 Stat. 2057 (2002). Though the Ninth Circuit later narrowed its decision, the Supreme Court granted a review to great fanfare. Then, as a great letdown to Court watchers, it dismissed the case on a procedural ground.

Thus, the questions remain about what the Constitution allows our government to state about God. Can government state there is a God—a fundamental, religious belief? Can government state that there is a singular God? Finally, can government define one aspect of the nature of God, namely, that our nation is under God, implying that God specially endorses the United States? Berger at 656.

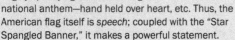

reading of the First Amendment.[6] Though Holmes gets the credit,[7] he was following Milton:

"Let her [Truth] and Falsehood grapple; who ever knew Truth put to the worse in a free and open encounter?"[8]

Holmes would have also known that Jefferson preached that the people

"may safely be trusted to hear everything true and false, and to form a correct judgment between them . . . ."[9]

If one reads Holmes's statement closely, however, he does not say that the free and open marketplace of ideas will always produce truth but only that it is "the best test of truth."[10]

After all, regarding both expression and belief, the ancient Athenian Demosthenes warned that

"it would be dangerous if there ever happened to coexist a considerable number of men who were bold and clever speakers, but full of . . . disgraceful wickedness. For the people would be led astray by them to make many mistakes."[11]

---

3. The American flag and invoking the national anthem are powerful symbols.

"O'er the ramparts we watch" (from the "Star Spangled Banner") in a 1945 recruiting poster

Saint images destroyed during the Reformation at the Cathedral of Saint Martin, Utrecht

Thus, it begs the question: When a person burns the flag is he *doing something* or *saying something*? If he is just *doing* something, the First Amendment does not protect him. But if he is *saying* something, it does. So far, despite calls from senators and lower court judges, the Supreme Court has affirmed that burning a flag in a political context is "speech," both "inherently" and "conventionally" expressive. *Rumsfeld v. Forum for Academic & Institutional Rights, Inc.*, 547 U.S. 47, 66 (2006); *Barnes v. Glen Theatre, Inc.*, 501 U.S. 560, 577 n.4 (1991) (Scalia, J., concurring in the judgment).

Burning flags as speech?

5. *Abrams v. United States*, 250 U.S. 616, 624–31 (1919) (Holmes, J., dissenting, joined by Brandeis, J.).

4. *Cohen v. California*, 403 U.S. 15 (1971) highlights both symbolic and written "speech." Mr. Cohen walked into a Los Angeles courthouse wearing a jacket inscribed with "Fuck the Draft." Writing for a 5-4 majority, the conservative justice John Marshall Harlan II wrote that "one man's vulgarity is another's lyric" and that in the context of opposing the Vietnam War, the "unseemly expletive" was used as a political protest. If Mr. Cohen can wear such a jacket in political protest, he most certainly can burn the same jacket as political speech. Thus, if he wears a jacket with the American flag, he could do the same.

6. Through various opinions, Holmes and Justice Louis Brandeis formed the foundation of modern free speech law. *See Whitney v. California*, 274 U.S. 357, 372–80 (1927) (Brandeis, J., concurring, joined by Holmes, J.); *United States v. Schwimmer*, 279 U.S. 644, 653–55 (1929) (Holmes, J., dissenting, joined by Brandeis, J.). These cases led to *Brandenburg v. Ohio*, 395 U.S. 444, 447 n.2, 449 (1969), punishing "mere advocacy" without "*incitement to imminent lawless action*" violates the First and Fourteenth Amendments. *Compare Stanley* Ingber, *The Marketplace of Ideas: A Legitimizing Myth*, 1984 Duke L.J. 1 (1984) (arguing that Holmes's marketplace is a flawed forum). Holmes may not always have been such a prophet of free speech. During World War I, he joined a more restrictive Court deciding the extent of the Espionage Act of 1917 and its 1918 amendments, where he wrote that even the "*most stringent protection of free speech would not protect a man in falsely shouting fire in a theatre and causing a panic.*" *Schenck v. United States*, 249 U.S. 47, 52 (1919).

Holmes

Brandeis

7. Holmes remains the most celebrated justice of all time, with his own stamp and even a movie (highly fictionalized), The Magnificent Yankee (MGM 1950).

8. AREOPAGITICA, *quoted in* Witte, *Milton*, at 1529, 1586; *see also* Werhan at 322.

9. *Quoted in* Jeremy D. Bailey, Thomas Jefferson and Executive Power 218 (2007).

10. John Stuart Mill regarded the premise that truth would trump falsehood in a free society as nothing more than "*a piece of idle sentimentality.*" John Stuart Mill, On Liberty (1859).

John Stuart Mill

11. *Quoted in* Werhan at 332.

Thus, the notion that what is true or best will win is not a given.[1]

A person's "truth" encompasses conscience and privacy, the very essence of what it means to live free. For the individual and society, what conscience and privacy mean evolves.

As the Framers designed it, the First Amendment allows for evolution.[2] The Framers addressed the future, not the past.[3] By any measure we have more freedom of speech and religion today. The World Wide Web, for instance, has given us greater scope than ever, and no state has an established religion.

But who is listening?

Do the media inform or lead with "*bold and clever speakers*"?[4] "The media" seeks to manipulate us every day, to influence who we vote for to the toothpaste we buy.[5] And the lines between advertising, entertainment, and news are often so blurred as to be indistinguishable.[6]

This is where religion comes in, not just in the sense of a specific religion like Catholic, Baptist, or Muslim, but more broadly to refer to a world view that provides fundamental values and understanding.

We need something to help see the lines between the messages we get. That something can be traditional religion, a code of ethics, a philosophy, or principles by which to live. In this sense, even an atheist can have "religion."

Protecting that religion from the government is the First Amendment.

As Justice Robert Jackson eloquently wrote,

> "[i]f there is any fixed star in our constitutional

---

1. Validating Demosthenes's warning is the documentary film, SHOUTING FIRE: STORIES FROM THE EDGE OF FREE SPEECH (Moxie Firecracker Films 2009), showing how both government and private interest groups can still violate the First Amendment's sprit, if not its letter.

Demosthenes

2. **A train ride that changed how we speak:** Holmes was riding a train with another famous Judge, Learned Hand, on June 19, 1918, between New York and Boston, and their conversation helped "shape" Holmes' views. *See* Gerald Gunther, *Learned Hand and the Origins of Modern First Amendment Doctrine: Some Fragments of History*, 27 STAN. L. REV. 719 (1975), (discussing Hand's 1917 decision in *Masses Publishing Co. v. Patten*, 244 F. 535 (S.D.N.Y. 1917), rev'd, 246 F. 24 (2d Cir. 1917), as a precursor of Holmes's opinions). *See also* Stephen M. Feldman, *Free Speech, World War I, and Republican Democracy: The Internal and External Holmes*, 6 FIRST AMEND. L. REV. 192 (2008) (discussing the scholarly debate on whether Holmes really changed his views on speech when comparing *Abrams* with his prior cases). Holmes also had read Zechariah Chafee, Jr., *Freedom of Speech in War Time*, 32 HARV. L. REV. 932 (1919). Chafee concluded that Framers like Madison intended "*to wipe out the common law of sedition and make further prosecutions for criticisms of the government, without any incitement to law-breaking, forever impossible in the United States.*" *Id.* at 947. Chafee (1885–1957) was an early free speech scholar and Harvard law professor who Senator Joseph McCarthy once pronounced "*dangerous*" at a 1952 U.S. Senate subcommittee hearing. *See* John Wertheimer, *Review: Freedom of Speech: Zechariah Chafee and Free-Speech History*, 22 REVS. IN AM. HIST. 365 (1994).

3. *See* Levy, *Free Press Clause*, at 180.

4. The 2004 presidential campaign showed how an organized media campaign could derail the candidacy of a decorated Vietnam War veteran. The Swift Boat Veterans for Truth had the sole purpose of questioning John Kerry's war record and helping derail his bid for president. A person can now be "swift-boated" as part of a political smear campaign.

The "Birthers" mounted a similar claim against President Barack Obama, claiming he was not born in the United States and therefore could not be president. The tabloids picked up on the myth as well as CNN's

Holmes   Chafee

Judge Billings Learned Hand (1872–1961) was a federal judge who served on the District Court for the Southern District of New York and later on the Second Circuit. Legal scholars and the Supreme Court have quoted Hand more often than any other lower court judge.

Swift Vets for Truth

constellation, it is that no official, high or petty, can prescribe what shall be orthodox in politics, nationalism, religion, or other matters of opinion or force citizens to confess by word or act their faith therein." [7]

So you can believe what you want and say what you want, and the government can't do anything to you—at least in theory.

Just two years after Jackson wrote the words quoted above, he dissented from the Supreme Court's decision that upheld interning all persons of Japanese ancestry, including almost 100,000 citizens, in concentration camps:

"A military order, however unconstitutional, is not apt to last longer than the military emergency . . . . But once a judicial opinion rationalizes such an order to show that it conforms to the Constitution . . . the Court for all time has validated the principle of racial discrimination in criminal procedure and of transplanting American citizens. The principle then lies about like a loaded weapon ready for the hand of any authority that can bring forward a plausible claim of an urgent need." [8]

Jackson articulated the great worry regarding expanding government power during an ill-defined "war on terror;" all it takes is *"a plausible claim of an urgent need* "to justify curtailing liberty." The collapse of the Twin Towers on September 11, 2001, created a plausible claim.[9]

Rights and the rule of law are fragile things in a violent world. In the face of *"plausible claims,"* freedom of speech, press, and religion are always at risk. So far, after a crisis has passed, they have tended to come out stronger.

But the future does not guarantee it.

Lou Dobbs, despite the fact that the state of Hawaii has released his birth certificate. The White House released the long version on April 27, 2011 to remove all doubt.

ama's birth certificate

5. We all grew up with *"Sticks and stones may break my bones, but words will never hurt me."*

A good enough lesson for children that most adults learn is not true. As the philosopher Jean-Paul Sartre wrote, *"Words are loaded pistols."*

Or as the Australian rock band INXS (pronounced as "In Excess") sings, *"Words are weapons shaper than knives, makes you wonder how the other half dies."*

Sartre

6. The film NETWORK (MGM 1976) showed how news can become entertainment and vice-versa. Peter Finch won a posthumous Oscar for playing Howard Beale, yelling *"I'm mad as hell, and I'm not going to take this anymore!"*

7. W. Va. Bd. of Educ. v. Barnette, 319 U.S. 624, 641–42 (1943).

8. *Korematsu v. United States*, 323 U.S. 214, 246 (1944), reh'g denied, 324 U.S. 885 (1945) (Jackson, J., dissenting).

Korematsu (finally) receiving the Presidential Medal of Freedom in 1998

Fred Korematsu was the original plaintiff challenging internment

9. The Twin Towers burning on 9/11.

Robert H. Jackson

BIBLIOGRAPHY

CASES:

ABRAMS V. UNITED STATES, 250 U.S. 616 (1919).

BARNES V. GLEN THEATRE, INC., 501 U.S. 560 (1991).

BRANDENBURG V. OHIO, 395 U.S. 444 (1969).

BRANDENBURG V. OHIO, 395 U.S. 444 (1969).

COHEN V. CALIFORNIA, 403 U.S. 15 (1971).

COUNTY OF ALLEGHENY V. ACLU, 492 U.S. 573 (1989).

DENNIS V. UNITED STATES, 341 U.S. 494 (1951).

EDWARDS V. AGUILLARD, 482 U.S. 578 (1987).

EPPERSON V. ARKANSAS, 393 U.S. 97 (1968).

EVERSON V. BOARD OF EDUCATION, 330 U.S. 1 (1947).

FREDERICK V. MORSE, 439 F.3D 1114 (9TH CIR. 2006).

GARLAND V. TORRE, 259 F.2D 545 (2D CIR. 1958).

GITLOW V. NEW YORK, 268 U.S. 652 (1925).

HOLY TRINITY CHURCH V. UNITED STATES, 143 U.S. 457 (1892).

HUSTLER MAGAZINE, INC. V. FALWELL, 485 U.S. 46 (1988).

JACOBELLIS V. OHIO, 378 U.S. 184 (1964).

KOREMATSU V. UNITED STATES, 323 U.S. 214 (1944), RH'G DENIED, 324 U.S. 885 (1945).

LAMONT V. POSTMASTER GENERAL, 381 U.S. 301 (1965).

LEE V. WEISMAN, 505 U.S. 577 (1992).

LYNCH V. DONNELLY, 465 U.S. 668 (1984).

MASSES PUBLISHING CO. V. PATTEN, 244 F. 535 (S.D.N.Y. 1917), REV'D, 246 F. 24 (2D CIR. 1917).

MCCREARY COUNTY V. ACLU OF KENTUCKY, 545 U.S. 844 (2005).

MCINTYRE V. OHIO ELECTIONS COMM'N, 514 U.S. 334 (1995).

MCLEAN V. ARKANSAS BOARD OF EDUCATION, 529 F. SUPP. 1255 (E.D. ARK. 1982).

MORSE V. FREDERICK, 551 U.S. 393 (2007).

NATIONAL ASS'N OF HOME BUILDERS V. DEFENDERS OF WILDLIFE, 551 U.S. 644 (2007).

NEAR V. MINNESOTA, 283 U.S. 697 (1931).

NEW YORK TIMES CO. V. U.S. (PENTAGON PAPERS), 403 U.S. 713 (1971).

NEW YORK TIMES V. SULLIVAN, 376 U.S. 254, 273 (1964).

NEWDOW V. U.S. CONGRESS (NEWDOW I) 292 F.3D 597 (9TH CIR 2002).

REYNOLDS V. UNITED STATES, 98 U.S. 145 (1878).

ROTH V. UNITED STATES, 354 U.S. 476 (1957).

RUMSFELD V. FORUM FOR ACADEMIC & INSTITUTIONAL RIGHTS, INC., 547 U.S. 47 (2006).

SCHENCK V. UNITED STATES, 249 U.S. 47 (1919).

SCOPES V. STATE, 278 S.W. 57 (TENN. 1925).

STATE V. BUCHANAN, 436 P.2D 729 (OR. 1968).

STATE V. KNOPS, 183 N.W.2D 93 (WIS. 1971).

STATE V. SCOPES, 152 TENN. 424 (TENN. 1925).

STROMBERG V. CALIFORNIA, 283 U.S. 359 (1931).

UNITED STATES V. SCHWIMMER, 279 U.S. 644 (1929).

Van Orden v. Perry, 545 U.S. 677 (2005).
Vidal v. Girard's Executors, 43 U.S. 127 (1844).
Wallace v. Jaffree, 472 U.S. 38 (1985).
Watts v. Indiana, 338 U.S. 49 (1949).
West Virgina Bd. of Educ. v. Barnette, 319 U.S. 624 (1943).
Whitney v. California, 274 U.S. 357 (1927).
Zorach v. Clauson, 343 U.S. 306 (1951).

CONSTITUIONS:

UNITED STATES CONSTITUTION

STATUTES:

36 U.S.C. § 301 (2006).
The Catholic Relief Act of 1829, 10 Geo. 4, c. 7 (Eng.).
The Ecclesiastical Appeals Act, 1532, 24 Hen. 8, c. 12.

BOOKS:

1 HISTORICAL COLLECTIONS: CONSISTING OF STATE PAPERS AND OTHER AUTHENTIC DOCU-
MENTS: INTENDED AS MATERIALS FOR A HISTORY OF THE UNITED STATES OF AMERICA
(Ebenezer Hazard ed., T. Dobson 1792).
3 JOSEPH STORY, COMMENTARIES ON THE CONSTITUTION OF THE UNITED STATES (1833).
4 WILLIAM BLACKSTONE, COMMENTARIES.
4 WILLIAM BLACKSTONE, COMMENTARIES (1769), reprinted in L. LEVY, FREEDOM OF THE
PRESS FROM ZENGER TO JEFFERSON (1966).
ALAN HAYNES, INVISIBLE POWER: THE ELIZABETHAN SECRET SERVICES 1570-1603 (1992).
ALF J. MAPP, THE FAITHS OF OUR FATHERS: WHAT AMERICA'S FOUNDERS REALLY BELIEVED
(2005).
ANN COULTER, GODLESS: THE CHURCH OF LIBERALISM (2006).
ANTHONY LEWIS, FREEDOM FOR THE THOUGHT THAT WE HATE: A BIOGRAPHY OF THE
FIRST AMENDMENT (2007).
ARISTOTLE, POETICS 1459A (McGill-Queen's University Press 1997).
ARTHUR MILLER, THE CRUCIBLE (1953).
Brent Tarter, Virginians and the Bill of Rights, in THE BILL OF RIGHTS: A LIVELY HERI-
TAGE (Jon Kukla ed. 1987).
BROOKE ALLEN, MORAL MINORITY: OUR SKEPTICAL FOUNDING FATHERS (2006).
CAMILLE SAINT-SAËNS, HENRY VIII (1883).
CATHERINE DRINKER BOWEN, MIRACLE AT PHILADEPHIA: THE STORY OF THE CONSTITU-
TIONAL CONVENTION MAY TO SEPTEMBER 1789 (1966).
CHARLES DICKENS, A CHILD'S HISTORY OF ENGLAND, Vol. III (1953) available at http://
www.archive.org/stream/childshistoryofe03dickrich#page/58/mode/2up (last visited
November 7, 2009).
COLIN RHYS LOVELL, ENGLISH CONSTITUTIONAL AND LEGAL HISTORY (1962).
CYNTHIA SUSAN CLEGG, CENSORSHIP IN JACOBEAN ENGLAND (2001).

CYNTHIA SUSAN CLEGG, PRESS CENSORSHIP IN ELIZABETHAN ENGLAND (1997).

DAN BROWN, THE DAVINCI CODE (2003).

DANNY DANZIGER & JOHN GILLINGHAM, 1215: THE YEAR OF MAGNA CARTA (2003).

DAVID HOWARTH, 1066: THE YEAR OF THE CONQUEST (1977).

DAVID L. HOLMES, THE FAITHS OF THE FOUNDING FATHERS (2006).

DAVID LOADES, POLITICS, CENSORSHIP AND THE ENGLISH REFORMATION (1991).

DAVID M. O'BRIEN, FREEDOM OF SPEECH AND FREE GOVERNMENT: THE FIRST AMENDMENT, THE SUPREME COURT AND THE POLITY, IN JON KUKLA, ED. THE BILL OF RIGHTS: A LIVELY HERITAGE (1987).

DAVID MCCULLOUGH, JOHN ADAMS (2001).

ENCYCLOPEDIA OF CATHOLICISM (RICHARD P. MCBRIEN, GEN. ED.) (1995).

E.R. CHAMBERLIN, THE BAD POPES (1969).

FLOYD ABRAMS, SPEAKING FREELY: TRAILS OF THE FIRST AMENDMENT (2005).

G.R. ELTON, THE TUDOR CONSTITUTION: DOCUMENTS AND COMMENTARY (1960).

GARRY WILLS, SAINT AUGUSTINE (1999).

GARY KOWALSKI, REVOLUTIONARY SPIRITS: THE ENLIGHTENED FAITH OF AMERICA'S FOUNDING FATHERS (2008).

GEOFFREY CHAUCER, THE CANTERBURY TALES (14TH C.).

GEOFFREY COWAN, THE PEOPLE V. CLARENCE DARROW: THE BRIBERY TRIAL OF AMERICA'S GREATEST LAWYER (1993).

GEOFFREY R. STONE, PERILOUS TIMES: FREE SPEECH IN WARTIME, FROM THE SEDITION ACT OF 1798 TO THE WAR ON TERRORISM (2004).

J. W. EHRLICH, THE HOLY BIBLE AND THE LAW (1962).

J. WILLIAM FROST, A PERFECT FREEDOM: RELIGIOUS LIBERTY IN PENNSYLVANIA (1990).

JAMES ALEXANDER, A BRIEF NARRATIVE OF THE CASE AND TRIAL OF JOHN PETER ZENGER, PRINTER OF THE NEW YORK WEEKLY JOURNAL (1963).

JANICE CONNELL, FAITH OF OUR FOUNDING FATHER: THE SPIRITUAL JOURNEY OF GEORGE WASHINGTON (2003).

JEREMY D. BAILEY, THOMAS JEFFERSON AND EXECUTIVE POWER 218 (2007).

JOHN AYTO, DICTIONARY OF WORD ORIGINS (1990).

JOHN FOXE, FOXE'S BOOK OF MARTYRS (1563).

JOHN GILLINGHAM, THE WARS OF THE ROSES (1981).

JOHN LE CARRE, A MURDER OF QUALITY (1962).

JOHN LE CARRE, CALL FOR THE DEAD (1961).

JOHN LE CARRE, SMILEY'S PEOPLE (1979).

JOHN LE CARRE, THE HONOURABLE SCHOOLBOY (1977).

JOHN LE CARRE, TINKER, TAILOR, SOLDIER, SPY (1974).

JOHN MILTON , AREOPAGITICA: A SPEECH OF MR. JOHN MILTON FOR THE LIBERTY OF UNLI-CENSED PRINTING TO THE PARLIAMENT OF ENGLAND (1644).

JOHN MILTON, PARADISE LOST (1667–68).

JOHN STUART MILL, ON LIBERTY (1859).

JON MEACHAM, AMERICAN GOSPEL: GOD, THE FOUNDING FATHERS, AND THE MAKING OF A NATION (2007).

JOSEPH J. ELLIS, HIS EXCELLENCY: GEORGE WASHINGTON (2004).

KURT VON S. KYNELL, SAXON AND MEDIEVAL ANTECEDENTS OF THE ENGLISH COMMON LAW (2000).

LARRY D. ELDRIDGE, A DISTANT HERITAGE: THE GROWTH OF FREE SPEECH IN EARLY AMERI-
CA (1994).

LEONARD W. LEVY, BILL OF RIGHTS IN ESSAYS ON THE MAKING OF THE CONSTITUTION (LEON-
ARD W. LEVY ED., 1987).

LEONARD W. LEVY, EMERGENCE OF A FREE PRESS (1985).

LEONARD W. LEVY, LEGACY OF SUPPRESSION (1960).

LEONARD W. LEVY, ORIGINS OF THE FIFTH AMENDMENT (1968).

MARK TWAIN, THE PRINCE AND THE PAUPER (1881).

MICHAEL FARRIS, FROM TYNDALE TO MADISON: HOW THE DEATH OF AN ENGLISH MARTYR
LED TO THE AMERICAN BILL OF RIGHTS, CH. 3 (2007).

NATHANIEL HAWTHORNE, THE SCARLET LETTER (1850).

PETER ACKROYD, THE LIFE OF THOMAS MORE (1999).

PETER BROWN, AUGUSTINE OF HIPPO (1967).

PLATO, APOLOGY 21D IN PLATO: COMPLETE WORKS (HACKETT, 1997) (G. M. A. GRUBE, TRANS,
REV C. D. C. REEVE, JOHN M. COOPER, ED.).

PLATO, LAWS 225 (R.G. BURY TRANS., HARVARD UNIVERSITY PRESS 1926) (N.D.).

PLATO, THE REPUBLIC, (TRANS. BENJAMIN JOWETT 2009) AVAILABLE AT HTTP://CLASSICS.MIT.EDU/
PLATO/REPUBLIC.HTML.

R. BLAIN ANDRUS, LAWYER: A BRIEF 5,000 YEAR HISTORY (2009).

RAY BRADBURY, FAHRENHEIT 451 (1951).

REBECCA L. MCMURRY & JAMES F. MCMURRY, JR. THE SCANDALMONGER AND THE NEWSPA-
PER WAR OF 1802 (2000).

RICH BEYER, THE GREATEST STORIES NEVER TOLD: 100 TABLES FROM HISTORY TO ASTON-
ISH, BEWILDER & STUPEFY (2003).

RICHARD BROOKHISER, WHAT WOULD THE FOUNDERS DO? (2006).

RICHARD MARIUS, THOMAS MORE: A BIOGRAPHY (1985).

ROBERT A. RUTLAND, FREEDOM OF THE PRESS, IN THE BILL OF RIGHTS: A LIVELY HERITAGE
(JOHN KUKLA ED., 1987).

ROBERT HENDRICKSON, QPB ENCYCLOPEDIA OF WORD AND PHRASE ORIGINS (2004).

RON CHERNOW, ALEXANDER HAMILTON (2004).

S. MUTCHOW TOWERS, CONTROL OF RELIGIOUS PRINTING IN EARLY STUART ENGLAND
(2003).

SAMUEL RUTHERFORD, LEX, REX, AVAILABLE AT THE LIBERTY LIBRARY OF CONSTITUTIONAL CLAS-
SICS, HTTP://WWW.CONSTITUTION.ORG/SR/LEXREX.HTM.

STEPHEN E. AMBROSE, D-DAY JUNE 6, 1944: THE CLIMACTIC BATTLE OF WORLD WAR II
(1994).

STEPHEN HESS & SANDY NORTHROP, DRAWN & QUARTERED: THE HISTORY OF AMERICAN
POLITICAL CARTOONS (1996).

STEVEN WALDMAN, FOUNDING FAITHS: HOW OUR FOUNDING FATHERS FORGED A RADICAL
NEW APPROACH TO RELIGIOUS LIBERTY (2009).

SUSAN FORD WILTSHIRE, GREECE, ROME, AND THE BILL OF RIGHTS (1992).

T.S. ELIOT, MURDER IN THE CATHEDRAL (1935).

THE BIBLE

THE FEDERALIST 44 (JAMES MADISON).

THE FEDERALIST 51 (JAMES MADISON).

THE WORKS OF FLAVIUS JOSPEHUS (TRANS. WILLIAM WHISTON 1847).

THE WORKS OF PLATO, APOLOGY 60 (IRWIN EDMAN ED., BENJAMIN JOWETT TRANS., RANDOM HOUSE 1956).

THOMAS CAHILL, HOW THE IRISH SAVED CIVILIZATION: THE UNTOLD STORY OF IRELAND'S HEROIC ROLE FROM THE FALL OF ROME TO THE RISE OF MEDIEVAL EUROPE (1995).

THOMAS JEFFERSON, THE JEFFERSON BIBLE: THE LIFE AND MORALS OF JESUS OF NAZARETH (2010).

THOMAS MORE, UTOPIA (1516).

THOMAS PAINE, THE AGE OF REASON: PART ONE (1794).

TIM F. LAHAYE, FAITH OF OUR FOUNDING FATHERS (1996).

UMBERTO ECO, THE NAME OF THE ROSE (1980).

WALTER SCOTT, REDGAUNTLET (1824).

WILL DURANT, THE AGE OF FAITH: A HISTORY OF MEDIEVAL CIVILIZATION – CHRISTIAN, ISLAMIC, AND JUDAIC – FROM CONSTANTINE TO DANTE: A.D. 325-1300 (1950).

WILLIAM BRADFORD, HISTORY OF PLYMOUTH PLANTATION (LITTLE, BROWN & CO. 1856).

WILLIAM H. REHNQUIST, GRAND INQUESTS: THE HISTORIC IMPEACHMENT S OF JUSTICE SAMUEL CHASE AND PRESIDENT ANDREW JOHNSON (1992).

WILLIAM ROPER, THE LIFE OF SIR THOMAS MORE C. 1556 57 (GERARD B. WEGEMER AND STEPHEN W. SMITH EDS. 2003) AVAILABLE AT HTTP://WWW.THOMASMORESTUDIES.ORG/DOCS/ROPER. PDF.

WILLIAM SHAKESPEARE, THE FAMOUS HISTORY OF THE LIFE OF KING HENRY THE EIGHTH (1613).

WILLIAM L. SHIRER, THE RISE AND FALL OF THE THIRD REICH: A HISTORY OF NAZI GERMANY (1950, 1960).

WILLIAM TYNDALE AND DAVID DANIELL, TYNDALE'S NEW TESTAMENT (1996).

ARTICLES:

ALBERT W. ALSCHULER & ANDREW G. DEISS, A BRIEF HISTORY OF THE CRIMINAL JURY IN THE UNITED STATES, 61 U. CHI. L. REV. 867 (1994).

ANUJ C. DESAI, THE TRANSFORMATION OF STATUTES INTO CONSTITUTIONAL LAW: HOW EARLY POST OFFICE POLICY SHAPED MODERN FIRST AMENDMENT DOCTRINE, 58 HASTINGS L.J. 671 (2007).

BARBARA A. PERRY, JEFFERSON'S LEGACY TO THE SUPREME COURT: FREEDOM OF RELIGION, 31 SUP. CT. HIST. 181 (2006).

BLAKE D. MORANT, LESSONS FROM THOMAS MORE'S DILEMMA OF CONSCIENCE: RECONCILING THE CLASH BETWEEN A LAWYER'S BELIEFS AND PROFESSIONAL EXPECTATIONS, 78 ST. JOHN'S L.REV. 965 (2004).

CHARLES P. SHERMAN, A BRIEF HISTORY OF IMPERIAL ROMAN CANON LAW, 7 CAL. L. REV. 93 (1918).

DANIEL J. SOLOVE, THE FIRST AMENDMENT AS CRIMINAL PROCEDURE, 82 N.Y.U. L. REV. 112 (2007).

DAVID A. ANDERSON, LEVY VS. LEVY, 84 MICH. L. REV. 777 (1986) (REVIEWING LEONARD W. LEVY, EMERGENCE OF A FREE PRESS (1985).

DAVID K. DEWOLF, TEN TORTURED WORDS, 85 DENV. U. L. REV. 443, (2007) (REVIEWING STEPHEN MANSFIELD, TEN TORTURED WORDS: HOW THE FOUNDING FATHERS TRIED TO PROTECT RELIGION IN AMERICA AND WHAT'S HAPPENED SINCE (2007).

DAVID L. WARDLE, REASON TO RATIFY: THE INFLUENCE OF JOHN LOCKE'S RELIGIOUS BELIEFS ON THE CREATION AND ADOPTION OF THE UNITED STATES CONSTITUTION, 26 SEATTLE U. L. REV. 291 (2002).

DAVID M. RABBAN, THE AHISTORICAL HISTORIAN: LEONARD LEVY ON FREEDOM OF EXPRESSION IN EARLY AMERICAN HISTORY, 37 STAN. L. REV. 795 (1985) (BOOK REVIEW).

DAVID M. RABBAN, THE EMERGENCE OF MODERN FIRST AMENDMENT DOCTRINE, 50 U. CHI. L. REV. 1205 (1983).

DIANA WOODHOUSE, UNITED KINGDOM: THE CONSTITUTIONAL REFORM ACT 2005 – DEFENDING JUDICIAL INDEPENDENCE THE ENGLISH WAY, 5 INT'L J. CONST. L. 153 (2007)

DINITIA SMITH, WRITERS AS PLUNDERERS; WHY DO THEY KEEP GIVING AWAY OTHER PEOPLE'S SECRETS? N.Y. TIMES, OCTOBER 24, 1998, AVAILABLE AT HTTP://WWW.NYTIMES.COM/1998/10/24/ BOOKS/WRITERS-AS-PLUNDERERS-WHY-DO-THEY-KEEP-GIVING-AWAY-OTHER-PEOPLE-S-SECRETS. HTML?SEC=
&SPON=&PAGEWANTED=2.

DOUGLAS LAYCOCK, "NONCOERCIVE" SUPPORT FOR RELIGION: ANOTHER FALSE CLAIM ABOUT THE ESTABLISHMENT CLAUSE, 26 VAL. U. L. REV. 37 (1992).

DOUGLAS LAYCOCK, TOWARDS A GENERAL THEORY OF THE RELIGION CLAUSES: THE CASE OF CHURCH LABOR RELATIONS AND THE RIGHT TO CHURCH AUTONOMY, 81 COLUM. L. REV. 1373 (1981).

ERIC SCHNAPPER, 'LIBELOU'" PETITIONS FOR REDRESS OF GRIEVANCES: BAD HISTORIOGRAPHY MAKES WORSE LAW, 74 IOWA L. REV. 303 (1989).

ERWIN CHEMERINSKY, HISTORY, TRADITION, THE SUPREME COURT, AND THE FIRST AMENDMENT, 44 HASTINGS L.J. 901 (1993).

EUGENE VOLOKH, SYMBOLIC EXPRESSION AND THE ORIGINAL MEANING OF THE FIRST AMENDMENT, 97 GEO. L.J. 1057 (2009).

GEOFFREY R. STONE, THE WORLD OF THE FRAMERS: A CHRISTIAN NATION? 56 UCLA L. REV. 1 (2008).

GERALD GUNTHER, LEARNED HAND AND THE ORIGINS OF MODERN FIRST AMENDMENT DOCTRINE: SOME FRAGMENTS OF HISTORY, 27 STAN L. REV. 719 (1975).

GREGORY C. DOWNS, RELIGIOUS LIBERTY THAT ALMOST WASN'T: ON THE ORIGIN OF THE ESTABLISH-MENT CLAUSE OF THE FIRST AMENDMENT, 30 U. ARK. LITTLE ROCK L. REV. 19 (2007).

HAROLD J. BERMAN, LAW AND BELIEF IN THREE REVOLUTIONS, 18 VAL. U. L. REV. 569 (1984).

HAROLD J. BERMAN, RELIGIOUS FOUNDATIONS OF LAW IN THE WEST: AN HISTORICAL PERSPECTIVE, 1 J.L. & RELIGION 3 (1983).

HAROLD W. WOLFRAM, JOHN LILBURNE,: DEMOCRACY'S PILLAR OF FIRE, 3 SYRACUSE L. REV. 213 (1952).

HERBERT W. TITUS, GOD'S REVELATION: FOUNDATION FOR THE COMMON LAW, 4 REGENT U. L. REV. 1 (1994).

HIRAD ABTAHI, REFLECTIONS ON THE AMBIGUOUS UNIVERSALITY OF HUMAN RIGHTS: CYRUS THE GREAT'S PROCLAMATION AS A CHALLENGE TO THE ATHENIAN DEMOCRACY'S PERCEIVED MONOPOLY ON HUMAN RIGHTS, 36 DENV. J. INT'L L. & POL'Y 55 (2007).

HUGO L. BLACK, THE BILL OF RIGHTS, 35 N.Y.U. L. REV. 865 (1960).

JACOB REYNOLDS, THE RULE OF LAW AND THE ORIGINS OF THE BILL OF ATTAINDER CLAUSE, 18 ST. THOMAS L. REV. 177 (2005).

JEFFREY K. SAWYER, BENEFIT OF CLERGY IN MARYLAND AND VIRGINIA, 34 AM. J. LEGAL HIST. 49 (1990).

JOHN WERTHEIMER, REVIEW: FREEDOM OF SPEECH: ZECHARIAH CHAFEE AND FREE-SPEECH HISTORY, 22 REVS. IN AM. HIST. 365 (1994).

JOHN WITTE, JR., "A MOST MILD AND EQUITABLE ESTABLISHMENT OF RELIGION": JOHN ADAMS AND THE MASSACHUSETTS EXPERIMENT, 41 J. CHURCH & ST. 213 (1999).

John Witte, Jr., Blest be the Ties that Bind: Covenant and Community in Puritan Thought, 36 Emory L.J. 579 (1987).

John Witte, Jr., Book Review, 16 J.L. & Religion 565 (2001) (reviewing Daniel L. Dreisbach, Religion and Politics in the Early Republic: Jasper Adams and the Church-State Debate (1996)).

John Witte, Jr., How to Govern a City on a Hill: The Early Puritan Contribution to American Constitutionalism, 39 Emory L.J. 41 (1990).

John Witte, Jr., Prophets, Priests, and Kings: John Milton and the Reformation of Rights and Liberties in England, 57 Emory L.J. 1527 (2008).

John Witte, Jr., Tax Exemption of Church Property: Historical Anomaly or Valid Constitutional Practice?, 64 S. Cal. L. Rev. 363 (1991).

Keith Werhan, The Classical Athenian Ancestry of American Freedom of Speech, 2008 Sup. Ct. Rev. 293 (2009).

Lael Daniel Weinberger, The Monument and the Message: Pragmatism and Principle in Establishment Clause Ten Commandments Litigation, 14 Tex. Wesleyan L. Rev. 393 (2008).

Leonard W. Levy, On the Origins of the Free Press Clause, 32 UCLA L. Rev. 177 (1984).

Leonard W. Levy, The Legacy Reexamined, 37 Stan. L. Rev. 767 (1985).

Mark J. Chadsey, Thomas Jefferson and the Establishment Clause, 40 Akron L. Rev. 623 (2007).

Martin E. Marty, Freedom of Religion and the First Amendment, in The Bill of Rights: A Lively Heritage 19 (Jon Kukla ed., 1987).

Martin E. Marty, On A Medial Moraine: Religious Dimensions Of American Constitutionalism 39 Emory L.J. 9 (1990).

Matthew C. Berger, Comment, One Nation Indivisible: How Congress's Addition of "Under God" to the Pledge of Allegiance Offends the Original Intent of the Establishment Clause, 3 U. St. Thomas L.J. 629 (2006).

Patrick M. Garry, The Myth of Separation: America's Historical Experience with Church and State, 33 Hofstra L. Rev. 475 (2004).

Richard Albert, Religion in the New Republic, 67 La. L. Rev. 1 (2006).

Robert A. Sedler, Essay: The Protection of Religious Freedom Under the American Constitution, 53 Wayne L. Rev. 817 (2007).

Robert Joseph Renaud & Lael Daniel Weinberger, Spheres Of Sovereignty: Church Autonomy Doctrine and the Theological Heritage of the Separation of Church and State, 35 N. Ky. L. Rev. 67 (2008).

Scott J. Street, Poor Richard's Forgotten Press Clause: How Journalists Can Use Original Intent to Protect their Confidential Sources, 27 Loy. L.A. Ent. L. Rev. 463 (2007).

Stanford E. Lehmberg, Parliamentary Attainder in the Reign of Henry VIII, 18 Hist. J. 675 (1975).

Stanley Ingber, The Marketplace of Ideas: A Legitimizing Myth, 1984 Duke L.J. 1 (1984).

Stephen M. Feldman, Free Speech, World War I, and Republican Democracy: The Internal and External Holmes, 6 First Amend. L. Rev. 192 (2008).

Steve Bachmann, Starting Again with the Mayflower . . . England's Civil War and America's Bill of Rights, 20 QLR 193 (2000).

Susanna Dokupil, "Thou Shalt Not Bear False Witness": "Sham" Secular Purposes in Ten Commandments Displays, 28 Harv. J.L. & Pub. Pol'y 609 (2005).

Susanna Frederick Fischer, Playing Poohsticks with the British Constitution? The Blair

GOVERNMENT'S PROPOSAL TO ABOLISH THE LORD CHANCELLOR, 24 PENN. ST. INT'L L. REV. 257 (2005).

THOMAS B. COLBY, A CONSTITUTIONAL HIERARCHY OF RELIGIONS? JUSTICE SCALIA, THE TEN COMMANDMENTS, AND THE FUTURE OF THE ESTABLISHMENT CLAUSE, 100 NW. U.L. REV. 1097 (2006).

THOMAS B. MCAFFEE, THE BILL OF RIGHTS, SOCIAL CONTRACT THEORY, AND THE RIGHTS "RETAINED" BY THE PEOPLE, 16 S. ILL. U. L.J. 267 (1992).

THOMAS JEFFERSON: ESTABLISHING A FEDERAL REPUBLIC, HTTP://WWW.LOC.GOV/EXHIBITS/JEFFERSON/JEFFFED.HTML (LAST VISITED NOVEMBER 20, 2009).

TREVOR D. DRYER, "ALL THE NEWS THAT'S FIT TO PRINT": THE NEW YORK TIMES, "YELLOW" JOURNALISM, AND THE CRIMINAL TRIAL 1898-1902, 8 NEV. L. J. 541 (2008).

WALTER B. HAMLIN, THE BILL OF RIGHTS OR THE FIRST TEN AMENDMENTS TO THE UNITED STATES CONSTITUTION, 68 COM. L. J. 233 (1963).

WILLIAM TRUNK, THE SCOURGE OF CONTEXTUALISM: CEREMONIAL DEISM AND THE ESTABLISHMENT CLAUSE, 49 B.C. L. REV. 571 (2008).

ZECHARIAH CHAFEE, JR., FREEDOM OF SPEECH IN WAR TIME, 32 HARV. L. REV. 932 (1919).

MOVIES:

300 (WARNER BROS. 2007).

A BRIDGE TOO FAR (UNITED ARTISTS 1977).

A KNIGHT'S TALE (COLUMBIA PICTURES 2001).

A MAN FOR ALL SEASONS (COLUMBIA PICTURES 1966).

A MAN FOR ALL SEASONS (TNT 1988).

AKEELAH AND THE BEE (LIONSGATE 2006).

ALL THE PRESIDENT'S MEN (WARNER BROS. 1976).

ANNE OF THE THOUSAND DAYS (UNIVERSAL PICTURES 1969).

BECKET (PARAMOUNT PICTURES 1964).

BEE SEASON (FOX SEARCHLIGHT PICTURES 2005).

BILL & TED'S EXCELLENT ADVENTURE (ORION PICTURES 1989).

BONNIE PRINCE CHARLIE (LONDON FILM PRODUCTIONS 1948).

BRAVEHEART (20TH CENTURY FOX 1995).

BRUCE ALMIGHTY (UNIVERSAL STUDIOS 2003).

CASINO ROYAL (METRO-GOLDWYN-MAYER 2006).

CITIZEN KANE (RKO PICTURES 1941).

CROMWELL (COLUMBIA PICTURES 1970).

ELIZABETH (GRAMERCY 1998).

EVAN ALMIGHTY (UNIVERSAL STUDIOS 2007).

EVER AFTER: A CINDERELLA STORY (20TH CENTURY FOX 1998).

EXCALIBUR (ORION PICTURES 1981).

FAHRENHEIT 451 (UNIVERSAL PICTURES 1966).

FROM RUSSIA WITH LOVE (UNITED ARTISTS 1963).

FROST/NIXON (UNIVERSAL STUDIOS 2008).

HENRY VIII (GRANADA TELEVISION 2003).

HOCUS POCUS (WALT DISNEY 1993).

INHERIT THE WIND (UNITED ARTISTS 1960).

JESUS CHRIST SUPERSTAR (UNIVERSAL STUDIOS 1973).

KING ARTHUR (TOUCHSTONE PICTURES 1994).

KINGDOM OF HEAVEN (20TH CENTURY FOX 2005).

LUTHER (MGM 2003).

MONTY PYTHON'S LIFE OF BRIAN (WARNER BROS. 1979).

NETWORK (MGM 1976).

OH, GOD (WARNER BROS. 1977).

PEOPLE V. LARRY FLYNT (COLUMBIA PICTURES 1996).

PLEASANTVILLE (NEW LINE CINEMA 1998).

QUEEN MARGOT (MIRAMAX 1994).

QUO VADIS (MGM 1951).

SEVEN (NEW LINE CINEMA 1995).

SHOUTING FIRE: STORIES FROM THE EDGE OF FREE SPEECH (MOXIE FIRECRACKER FILMS 2009).

THE 300 SPARTANS (20TH CENTURY FOX 1962).

THE CROW (MIRAMAX 1989).

THE DAVINCI CODE (COLUMBIA PICTURES 2006).

THE DAY AFTER TOMORROW (20TH CENTURY FOX 2004).

THE DEVIL'S ADVOCATE (WARNER BROS. 1997).

THE HOAX (MIRAMAX FILMS 2006).

THE LAST TEMPTATION OF CHRIST (UNIVERSAL STUDIOS 1988).

THE LION IN WINTER (UNIVERSAL PICTURES 1968).

THE LOVERS (LES AMANTS) (ZENITH INTERNATIONAL FILMS 1958).

THE MAGNIFICENT YANKEE (METRO-GOLDWYN-MAYER 1950).

THE MOST DANGEROUS MAN IN AMERICA: DANIEL ELLSBERG AND THE PENTAGON PAPERS (FIRST RUN FEATURES 2009).

THE MISSION (WARNER BROS. 1986).

THE NAME OF THE ROSE (20TH CENTURY FOX 1986).

THE OTHER BOLEYN GIRL (COLUMBIA PICTURES 2008).

THE PAPER (UNIVERSAL PICTURES 1994).

THE PASSION OF THE CHRIST (NEWMARKET FILMS 2004).

THE PRINCE AND THE PAUPER (1937).

THE PRINCE AND THE PAUPER (BUENA VISTA PICTURES 1990).

THE PRIVATE LIFE OF HENRY VIII (UNITED ARTISTS 1933).

THE PROPHECY (DIMENSION FILMS 1995).

THE SCARLET LETTER (HOLLYWOOD PICTURES 1995).

THE SENTINEL (UNIVERSAL PICTURES 1977).

THE STAR CHAMBER (20TH CENTURY FOX 1983).

THE TEN COMMANDMENTS (PARAMOUNT PICTURES 1923).

THE TEN COMMANDMENTS (PARAMOUNT PICTURES 1956).

THE TUDORS (SHOWTIME 2007-PRESENT).

MISC.:

ABRAHAM LINCOLN, SECOND INAUGURAL ADDRESS (MARCH 4, 1865).

ACT OF SUPREMACY, 1534, 26 HEN. 8, C. 1, AVAILABLE AT HTTP://TUDORHISTORY.ORG/PRIMARY/ SUPREMACY.HTML (LAST VISITED 10 FEBRUARY 2006).

AMNESTY INTERNATIONAL, CHINA: NO INVESTIGATION, NO REDRESS AND STILL NO FREE-DOM OF SPEECH! HUMAN RIGHTS ACTIVISTS TARGETED FOR DISCUSSING THE TIANANMEN CRACKDOWN, HTTP://WWW.AMNESTY.ORG/EN/LIBRARY/INFO/ASA17/025/2010/EN (LAST VISITED AUGUST 15, 2010).

HEINRICH HEINE, ALMANSOR: A TRAGEDY (1823).

MONTY PYTHON, OLIVER CROMWELL, ON MONTY PYTHON SINGS (VIRGIN RECORDS 1991).

THE CATHOLIC ENCYCLOPEDIA, HTTP://WWW.NEWADVENT.ORG/CATHEN/ (LAST VISITED JUNE 12, 2010).

THE PRINCE AND THE PAUPER (CLASSIC COMICS ISSUE 29 1946).

TREATY OF PEACE AND FRIENDSHIP BETWEEN THE UNITED STATES OF AMERICA AND THE BEY AND SUBJECTS OF TRIPOLI OF BARBARY, ART. XI (NOV. 4, 1796) AVAILABLE AT HTTP:// WWW.YALE.EDU/ LAWWEB/AVALON/DIPLOMACY/BARBARY/BAR1796T.HTM (LAST VISITED OCT. 14, 2006).

UNITED STATES HOLOCAUST MEMORIAL MUSEUM HTTP://WWW.USHMM.ORG/RESEARCH/LIBRARY/ FAQ/DETAILS.PHP?TOPIC=06#QUOTE_HEINE (LAST VISITED AUGUST 21, 2010).

WIKIPEDIA, HTTP://EN.WIKIPEDIA.ORG/WIKI/LORD_HIGH_CHANCELLOR.

CPSIA information can be obtained
at www.ICGtesting.com
Printed in the USA
BVOW05s1352300817
493528BV00011B/77/P